HUNGRy FOR THAT

HUNGRY FOR THAT

RECIPES FROM THE BEATBOX KITCHEN

RAPH RASHID

hardie grant books

MELBOURNE · LONDON

CONTENTS

This book is dedicated to my mother, Lesley Anne Philips, and my father, Abdul Rashid (RIP), an artist who just loved to work, paint, sing and cook.

INTRODUCTION

In the late nineties, I got hooked on two things: burgers and tacos. I was in the States trying to find buyers for the T-shirt label I'd started in Melbourne with my mate Danny, while at the same time interviewing and photographing music producers for a book called Behind the Beat. My two projects saw me travelling all across the country, photographing producers like DJ Shadow, DJ Premier and J Dilla, and being invited into all sorts of awesome, creative spaces. Along the way I got to sample burgers and tacos from all over the States, and I was totally blown away.

In Australia, where I was from, 'tacos' were the hard-shell variety that came in all-in-one meal kits, and burgers were made of tasteless beef covered in tomato sauce. I was amazed to discover how flavoursome the tacos and burgers could be.

I ate at small diners, street food stalls and food trucks and was frequently impressed by the freshness and simplicity of these foods. Most of all, I loved that it wasn't pretentious. Along the way, I met a lot of great people who were flipping burgers and making tacos – which was considered low-skilled, boring work – with pride. Their attention to detail and commitment to cooking great food honestly inspired me. It wasn't long before I was spending more time daydreaming about burgers and tacos than I was thinking about my business – or anything else for that matter.

*

Like most people, my love of food started during my childhood. My father was food obsessed, and he would make dinner for the whole family in around 30–45 minutes. We bonded over food. On Sunday nights, he would take me out for pizza after dinner, at around 10 pm.

My father came to Australia from Malaysia in 1968 on a Malaysian government scholarship.

The idea was that he would study and graduate abroad then take back his learned skills to work in Malaysia. Good theory, but what my father found in Australia was more than he ever could have imagined. He had left a small village in Malaysia and was now set free in Melbourne – a democratic metropolis – and quickly adjusted to balancing study and partying. He loved music, painting and cooking and, in Australia, he could indulge all of those passions. He dropped out of his town-planning course to study teaching at a college in Prahran. For his final prac' exam, he served up baskets of Malaysian-style fried chicken. His teachers bugged out as they had never tasted turmeric before – of course, he passed with flying colours. He fell in love with my mum and I was born in 1976.

We would travel to Malaysia every few years. We moved there for a while, but Australia had so much more opportunity and we ended up moving back after a year. We lived above our Malay restaurant and my father would teach high-school students during the day then come back and cook all night. I had no concept of how insane this was until I started working as a teenager. The restaurant put a lot of strain on my parents; they did a good job of keeping it together. Inevitably, though, it got the better of them and they decided to sell up and simplify things a bit.

A few years later, my father got the restaurant itch again and gave it another blast. With a friend, he opened up a new Malay restaurant. I was his dishwasher on Friday and Saturday nights. I loved it but, after a couple of years, there was a fallout with finances again and it was over. My father never cared too much about financial pressure, but it took its toll on my mum. I would see her upset and I remember thinking that I really wanted to protect her from financial stresses. Even though the burden of running a restaurant tore my parents apart, I still loved restaurants and couldn't understand why they didn't work – but I assumed that if they had worked, my pops would have gotten bored with them and tried something else.

Having caught my dad's food obsession, my first job outside of the family restaurant was making toffee apples at age 13. I had to put the sticks into the base of apples before they got dipped in toffee. My workstation consisted of an electric frying pan with melted wax, a crate of granny smith apples and a box of sticks. You had to dunk the sticks in the hot wax just deep enough so the wax ran over the tips of your fingers, then push the stick into the core of the apple. Payment was 60 cents per crate, and each one took about 30 minutes to fill. It was brutal but I didn't care – I was working and loving it. When I was 15, I went to work at a sandwich bar. It was awesome – until the owner got arrested for robbing all the neighbouring shops.

A year later, I dropped out of school and started working as a kitchen hand. I hated it. I was horrified by what I saw – the lasagne left in the bain marie at the end of the day was pushed down to form the base of the next day's lasagne! I was so shocked, I just split after a couple of weeks.

The experience put me off working in kitchens so much that I decided to study audio engineering. I loved music and had been DJ'ing and playing in rap groups for a few years. Out of audio school I made a few dollars around town by playing gigs. I went back to Malaysia to work in a studio, recording Malay pop artists, but I became obsessed with the local satay stand. I would meet my friends there to hang out – I loved the fire, the smell of the satay cooking over charcoal, the buzz in the atmosphere. Before long, I was spending more time there than I did at work. I quickly realised studio recording wasn't for me either.

I came back to Australia in 1994 and bumped into a good friend Danny at the train station. Danny and I were both into graffiti; we got talking and decided we should start making T-shirts together. Our label was called Blank. Danny and I moved into a sharehouse and we would print tees together during the day. At night, I would cook dinner for everyone, then we'd kick out some jams in our band room for hours. By the end of the nineties, our label was really starting to take off. We were selling as many T-shirts as we could print, and we were getting interest from the UK and the US.

I headed over to the US with my favourite lady in the whole world – my girlfriend, Beci Orpin – and we ate our way across the country. It was on that trip that I realised how incredible burgers and tacos could be. It was the trip that changed everything.

*

Soon after Beci and I returned home, we got married. Our first son Tyke was born and I started to travel a little less. That gave me time to hone my burger skills. I had no real plans to open a shop but I was acting like I did. I was chatting with bakers and butchers and they all started asking me when my shop was opening up. They didn't want to start working on samples until I knew what I was doing. The problem was I couldn't answer them – I didn't know.

One night at the pub, I bumped into my friend Woody. He was the band booker for a local music festival, and I mentioned to him that I wanted to do a burger stand somewhere. He said, 'Why don't you come up and do something at the festival?' I thought, 'Why not?'

I started researching equipment to buy and to hire. It was getting expensive and was going to be super time-consuming. I thought to myself, 'Okay, so I need to hire a truck, pick up all of this gear, get health department approval, set up a marquee, unload the truck, only to then have to pack it all back into the truck at the end.' My next thought was the clincher, 'Why don't I just fix everything in the truck and cut a service hatch out the side?' I now had a plan, but no cash. I chatted with some close buddies and four of them kicked me 10K each. They all put the money in because they thought I was crazy (in a good way). I made it happen, got the truck built and what happened next was close to the edge of insanity.

The newly finished truck arrived at 11 pm on the eve of the three-day festival. I had never driven a manual before, let alone a truck, and there

I was hopping along the freeway, revving and riding the hell out of the clutch, working it out as I went along. I arrived at the festival, which was situated two hours from Melbourne, and started setting up, only to discover the truck had faulty power circuits. The festival electricians worked through the night to get it sorted. My plan was to sell burgers and ice cream sandwiches made of warmed chocolate brownies with vanilla ice cream in between. I had lined up a few staff but it was a pretty casual arrangement. I just told them to come past and, if we needed help, then to jump in. I opened the hatch for the first time and, boom, it was on. Within about two hours we had to close. We just couldn't keep up with the constant stream of orders.

For the next two days, we continued to open and close; it was a bit like a wounded tennis player hitting some okay shots but never hitting a winner. My staff were great but not always around. On the second day I checked on my freezer. It had short-circuited, and all our ice cream (and profits) had melted away. It was heartbreaking. By day three I had slept a total of six hours. I was dying but soldiering on. The festival wound up and I put the takings in the safe. We packed up, pulled out and started driving back home. I took a wrong turn and needed to turn around. I kept driving for another 10 minutes before a car that was passing me indicated to me that my side hatch was open. What? I looked in the rear-view mirror and, sure enough, it was wide open. 'Hmm, that's weird,' I thought. I got out and closed it and thought nothing of it. Another half hour down the road, I started to nod off. I turned up the music, and begged my co-pilot for some conversation.

Then I had a sudden realisation. I halted. I jumped out and ran to the back of the truck to find that the unfastened safe with my takings enclosed was no longer there. In fact, it had flown off the shelf while I was making the U-turn and had bashed open the hatch and fallen out onto the road somewhere along the way.

Delirious, I turned the truck around and travelled back to the spot where I had made the U-turn, praying that it would be there. Sure enough, there it was, sitting up with the takings intact, like a pot of gold at the end of a very traumatic rainbow. I collapsed in the field, looking up at the sky and thought, 'This is a good omen. This is what I am supposed to be doing.'

It was 2009 when Beatbox Kitchen was born. There was no food truck scene in Melbourne at the time, but business grew organically. We set out to make the best burgers we could. We wanted to keep things simple and our customers seemed to love the freshness of the food. We created a sense of community by parking near an unused communal space. People would line up with their mates, order burgers, then all sit and eat in the park together. We felt blessed.

In 2011, my good friend BT and I started a Taco Truck to share our favourite tacos. We now have two Beatbox Kitchen trucks and two Taco Trucks that set-up shop all over Melbourne, all day every day, come rain, hail or shine.

THE ESSENTIALS

Before my parents would let me operate the gas stove – when I was around age 11 – I was allowed to use the electric sandwich maker. I started with the standard sandwich – grilled cheese – then moved on to baked beans etc. But then I needed more. Before too long I was loading the sandwich maker with all types of stuff. I was frying eggs, then I started to grill chicken in it, then I moved on to skewered meats. I really pushed that thing as hard as I could and, in many ways, its principles have stuck with me throughout the years – the limitations in gear both then and now in my food trucks have pushed me to be more creative.

I never had fancy pots and pans when I started to cook and you definitely don't need any for the recipes in this book. I am lucky that over the years I have managed to score some great pots, pans and knives from family and friends as gifts. However, as great as they are, by no means do they dictate the way I cook.

A couple of cheap assets for the kitchen are the tortilla press and a cast-iron frying pan. The cast iron can really take the heat, which is great for tortillas and also getting great colour into your food.

TORTILLA PRESS

MAKING CORN TORTILLAS

Tortillas start as dried field corn kernels, which are put through a process called nixtamalisation. The kernels are cooked in a lime solution at just below boiling point, then steeped in the same solution. The corn is then ground into fresh flour for tortillas. The taste of tortillas made from freshly ground corn is amazing. At home I use masa, prepared corn maize flour, to make my tortilla dough.

You can make corn tortillas using a rolling pin, but you get better results using a tortilla press. You can buy good cast-iron tortilla presses online or for a reasonable price from Mexican food retailers. If you've never used a tortilla press before it can seem a bit tricky, but it's actually really easy. A tortilla press is a simple device – two flat plates with a hinge at one side and a lever on the other side to press the plates together.

USING A TORTILLA PRESS

Once you've made your dough, open up the tortilla press and put down a sheet of baking paper on the base plate. Put the ball of dough in the centre, cover with another sheet of baking paper, then use the lever to press down on the dough. One side of the tortilla will probably be slightly thicker than the other, so open up the press again, rotate the tortilla 180 degrees, and gently press down again to even out the tortilla. Carefully peel off the top layer of baking paper and turn the tortilla into your palm, then peel away the other layer of baking paper.

Tortillas are traditionally cooked on a comal – a flat, cast-iron griddle – but a non-stick frying pan is fine to use at home. Heat the pan to medium and cook the tortillas for about a minute on each side then construct your tacos, burritos, enchiladas etc., as desired!

CHILLIES

With the growth of new cuisines in Australia, we are now finding many more varieties of fruit and vegetables being grown or imported. I am particularly happy with the quality of some of the dried chillies that are arriving. We also have some great farms growing really nice habañeros and jalapeños.

Growing up, I found that chillies were either super hot or not hot at all. The finer characteristics were not something I ever thought about until I started travelling and became mesmerised by the smell of fresh and dried chillies in markets around the world.

The names of most Mexican chillies change depending on whether they are fresh or dried. The jalapeño, for example, becomes a chipotle when it is smoked and dried. Here are some notes on the chillies I use in my recipes. You can order the dried chillies from lots of online retailers across the world.

JALAPEÑO

You're probably already familiar with the jalapeño. Most supermarkets sell jars of pickled jalapeños, which are great in burgers, tacos and pretty much anything you want to add a spicy kick to. Fresh jalapeños are a vibrant green but change to a deep red when fully ripe and are great in fresh salsas and salads. I've often seen fresh jalapeños, when they're in season, at the local supermarket – so keep an eye out for them.

CHIPOTLE

A chipotle is a dried, smoked jalapeño. Chipotles have an awesome, intensely smoky aroma and flavour and, using just a little, can add amazing depth to a dish.

CHIPOTLE EN ADOBO

Chipotle en adobo is simply a chipotle marinated in a tomato-based sauce – but the flavour is out of this world. It's smoky, spicy, rich, earthy, tomatoey – and a small amount is all you need to transform a dish.

HABAÑERO

The habañero is a legend among chillies – it's one of the hottest chillies in the world. Habañeros are so fiery that your hands will burn for days if you don't use gloves when preparing them – so make sure you do. They also have quite a fruity, citrusy flavour so they can really lift a salsa.

GUAJILLOS

Guajillos are dried mirasol chillies. Waxy-skinned and reddish/burgundy in colour, they're used in all sorts of Mexican dishes. With a moderate heat and earthy, slightly tart flavour, they add another dimension to sauces and cooked salsas.

ANCHOS

These meaty, deep reddish-brown chillies are hot, but also quite sweet. They're dried poblano chillies, and are one of the most commonly used chillies in Mexican dishes.

CHILE DE ÁRBOL

Chile de árbol is a super-hot, long, thin red chilli. It's often ground up and used in condiments, seasonings and salsas.

THE BASICS

I get a lot of satisfaction from making the simplest things that most people take for granted. The level of difficulty or the time involved becomes irrelevant when dealing with basic items like bread and tortillas. Sure, it's easier and probably cheaper to go to the shop and buy them, but where's the fun in that? Dipping a homemade corn chip or French fry into your favourite salsa will bring you a lot of satisfaction, I guarantee it!

BREAD

Makes **8** buns

2¼ teaspoons **dried yeast**

1 tablespoon **sugar**

600 g (1 lb 5 oz/4 cups)
plain (all-purpose) flour

2 teaspoons **salt**

250 ml (8½ fl oz/1 cup)
full-cream (whole) milk

2 tablespoons **vegetable
oil**

Using an electric mixer or food processor, combine the yeast, sugar and 75 ml (2½ fl oz) warm water until the yeast has dissolved. Let stand for about 15–20 minutes, or until the mixture starts to foam.

Add the flour, salt, milk, vegetable oil and 190 ml (6½ fl oz/¾ cup) warm water to the yeast mixture and mix with a dough hook attachment for 8–9 minutes, or until the dough is smooth. Transfer to a lightly oiled bowl, cover and set aside in a warm place for about 1 hour, or until the dough has doubled in size.

Preheat the oven to 180°C (350°F). Line a baking tray with baking paper.

Knock back the dough and knead it by hand for about 2–3 minutes, or until the dough is smooth and elastic. Divide the dough into 8 equal-sized portions and shape each into a round. Arrange the portions on the baking tray, leaving at least 5–6 cm (2–2½ in) between them. Cover and set aside to rise in a warm place for about 1 hour, or until doubled again in size. Bake the buns in the oven for 25–30 minutes, or until they sound hollow when tapped on the base. To help form a nice crust, use a spray bottle to lightly spray some water into the oven every 3–4 minutes while the bread is baking.

It's funny how we take a good bread roll for granted; I know I did. It took me three months to find the right baker to make Beatbox Kitchen's burger buns, and then another six months to get the bread right. Even now, if the weather is dramatically different from one day to the next – for example super freezing after being super hot – I will call the baker to check that he has taken it into consideration ... of course, he always has! I think this is what I love most about bread – it's a living thing that needs time and respect. Here is my favourite base bread recipe.

CORN TORTILLAS

Makes *10* tortillas
(11 cm/4¼ in, in diameter)

Using a fork, mix together the masa and 250 ml (8½ fl oz/1 cup) water in a bowl until well combined. It should be the consistency of Play-Doh. Portion the dough into 10 equal-sized balls.

Open your tortilla press and cover the base with baking paper. Place a ball of dough in the centre and cover with another sheet of baking paper. Use the handle to firmly close the tortilla press. Open the press, turn the tortilla 180 degrees and gently press again to even out the thickness of the tortilla. Peel off the top layer of baking paper and flip the tortilla into your palm. Gently peel away the other layer of baking paper.

To cook the tortillas, heat a non-stick frying pan over medium heat. Cook each tortilla for 1 minute on each side, or until the dough is cooked through. Transfer to a plate and cover with a damp, clean tea towel (dish towel) to keep warm. Repeat with the remaining dough.

150 g (5½ oz/1¼ cups) **masa harina**

Recipe note: You can also make the tortillas with a rolling pin. Lay a piece of baking paper on a flat working surface and put the ball of dough in the centre. Cover with more baking paper, then roll out with a rolling pin to create a tortilla about 11 cm (4¼ in) in diameter.

FLOUR TORTILLAS

Makes **20** tortillas
(11 cm/4¼ in, in diameter)

Combine the ingredients in a food processor. With the motor running, slowly add 250 ml (8½ fl oz/1 cup) warm water. Once the dough has come together, check the consistency. It should be the consistency of Play-Doh. If it's a bit sticky, add a touch more flour; if it's a bit dry, add a touch more warm water.

Portion the dough into 20 equal-sized balls. Cover with a clean tea towel (dish towel) and let them rest for 30 minutes.

Lay a piece of baking paper on a flat working surface and put a ball of dough in the centre. Cover with more baking paper, then roll out with a rolling pin to create a tortilla about 11 cm (4¼ in) in diameter.

To cook the tortillas, heat a non-stick frying pan over low–medium heat. Cook the tortillas for 1 minute on each side, or until the dough is cooked through. Transfer to a plate and cover with a damp, clean tea towel to keep warm. Repeat with the remaining dough balls.

100 g (3½ oz) **vegetable shortening** or **Copha**, cut into smallish chunks

500 g (1 lb 2 oz/3⅓ cups) **plain (all-purpose) flour**

10 g (⅓ oz) **salt**

1 quantity **Corn tortillas**
(pages 26-27)

cottonseed or **canola oil**
for deep-frying

Left-over corn tortillas are best turned into chips. It's best to use day-old tortillas.

CORN CHIPS

Serves **4** as a snack

Cut the tortillas into your desired corn (tortilla) chip shape.

In a deep-fryer or heavy-based saucepan, heat the oil to 175–180°C (345–350°F), or until a cube of bread dropped into the oil turns golden brown in 15 seconds.

Fry the tortilla pieces for about 1 minute, or until crispy. Be careful not to overcook as they will become bitter.

Serve with your favourite dip.

1 kg (2 lb 3 oz) **potatoes**
(russet burbank, kestrel,
sebago or other white-
fleshed potatoes are
best), unpeeled

1½ tablespoons **vinegar**

1 tablespoon **salt**

oil for deep-frying

sea salt for sprinkling

*What can I say? Fries are my favourite thing in the world.
I like to make them in small batches, to ensure my oil stays
hot and my fries turn out crisp.*

*This method allows you to freeze halfway, so you can always
have amazing fries ready to go.*

FRIES

Serves **4**

Cut the potatoes into long shoestring fries. In a saucepan,
combine the vinegar, salt and 1.5 litres (51 fl oz/6 cups) water
and bring to the boil. Cook half of the shoestring fries for
10 minutes then drain and refresh under cool water. Spread
them out on a tea towel (dish towel) to dry.

Repeat with the remaining shoestring fries.

Heat the oil in a deep-fryer, heavy-based saucepan or wok
to 180°C (350°F), or until a cube of bread dropped into
the oil turns golden brown in 15 seconds. Working in small
batches, cook the fries for 1 minute, then remove and drain
on paper towel. Repeat until you've done a first fry on all of
the shoestrings.

Leave the fries to cool at room temperature for about
30 minutes. At this point the fries can be bagged and frozen.
Cooking frozen fries will give a fluffier inside, but if you are
too hungry you can go straight for the final fry.

Preheat the oven to 180°C (350°F).

Bring the oil temperature back up to 180°C (350°F).
Again working in small batches, fry the shoestrings for
2–3 minutes, or until golden brown. Transfer the cooked fries
to a wire rack in the oven to keep them hot and crisp. Repeat
with the remaining fries.

Sprinkle with sea salt and serve.

PARTY STARTERS

As much as I love a big bag of potato crisps emptied into a bowl, I do find it a bit of a risky way to start a party. Crisps make me anti-social; they bring out a one-track mind that is not pretty. Too many times has Beci nudged me and whispered under her breath in a stern voice, 'Dude, lay off the crisps.' Take my advice – make something delicious that your guests will love. Get the party started right.

I like to make my guacamole with a mortar and pestle and a wooden spoon. I leave small chunks of avo in the mix, and little pieces of white onion to give it a little crunch, too.

CORN CHIPS WITH GUACAMOLE

Serves **4** as an appetiser

1 quantity **Corn chips** (page 30)

GUACAMOLE

½ **white onion**

½ teaspoon **sea salt**

1 **garlic clove**

3 large, ripe **avocados**, stoned

handful of **coriander (cilantro) leaves and stems**, finely chopped

lime juice to taste

finely ground **black pepper**

For the guacamole, finely dice half of the onion and set aside.

Using a large mortar and pestle, work together the sea salt, garlic and the remaining onion into a paste. Add the avocados and smash with the back of a wooden spoon until the avocado is mashed but still a little chunky.

Add the diced onion, coriander, a squeeze of lime juice and black pepper to taste. Combine well and serve with the corn chips.

These are my three favourite sauces to have with fries. Annie is the person who makes all the tomato relish we use in the trucks. The original recipe was given to her in '74 and has stood the test of time. Toum is a 'gangster garlic dip' – you must show respect. Add the oil too fast and it will split. Take your time and drizzle in the oil nice and slow, in a stream no thicker than a piece of dried linguine. The white sauce reminds me of eating fries with salt and vinegar as a kid. It also goes great with grilled chicken.

FRIES WITH 3 SAUCES

Serves **4** as an appetiser

1 quantity **Fries**
(see page 31)

ANNIE'S TOMATO RELISH
(see Recipe note)

1 kg (2 lb 3 oz) ripe
tomatoes

2 large **brown onions,**
chopped

1 tablespoon **salt**

700 ml (23½ fl oz)
malt vinegar

½ teaspoon **ground**
coriander

½ teaspoon **ground cumin**

½ teaspoon **ground**
turmeric

¼ teaspoon **ground**
fenugreek

¼ teaspoon **ground**
fennel seed

¼ teaspoon **ground**
cinnamon

¼ teaspoon freshly ground
black pepper

340 g (12 oz) **sugar**

2 teaspoons **sago**

2 **kaffir lime leaves**

2 teaspoons **mustard powder**

To make Annie's tomato relish, scald the tomatoes with boiling water, then put them under cold running water and rub off the skins. Chop the tomatoes and combine them with the onion in a bowl. Sprinkle with the salt and let stand overnight. The next day, drain the liquid.

Transfer the drained tomato mixture to a saucepan. Add the malt vinegar and bring to the boil over medium heat. Cook for 15 minutes, then add the remaining ingredients and boil for a further 45 minutes.

Remove the saucepan from the heat and use a hand-held blender or a food processor to blitz the relish to your desired consistency. Bottle in sterilised jars while the relish is hot. Let cool at room temperature, then refrigerate.

Recipe note: This recipe makes about 1 litre (34 fl oz/4 cups) of Annie's tomato relish. Keep any leftovers in the fridge to use on burgers, or anything else that goes great with relish.

TOUM

1 **garlic bulb** (about ½ cup garlic cloves), peeled

1 tablespoon **salt**

500 ml (17 fl oz/2 cups) **grapeseed oil**

80 ml (2½ fl oz/⅓ cup) **lemon juice**

To make the toum, pulse the garlic with the salt in a food processor until roughly chopped. With the motor running, add 125 ml (4 fl oz/½ cup) of the oil in a slow, steady stream. The garlic will begin to emulsify.

With the motor still running, drizzle in 1 tablespoon of the lemon juice.

Slowly add another 125 ml (4 fl oz/½ cup) of the oil, then another 1 tablespoon of the lemon juice. Repeat with the remaining oil and lemon juice until well combined.

WHITE SAUCE

60 g (2 oz/¼ cup) **mayonnaise**

60 ml (2 fl oz/¼ cup) **apple cider vinegar**

2 teaspoons cracked **black pepper**

pinch of **cayenne pepper**

1 teaspoon **lemon juice**

To make the white sauce, whisk together all of the ingredients.

Serve the three sauces with hot fries.

FRIED TOMATOES WITH APPLE SLAW

Serves **4**

I like to make this as a little intro dish for a dinner party. My friend Misha showed me how to tempura tomatoes years ago, and it's a real fine line between having too much batter and it slipping off and having not enough. The right batter consistency will coat the tomato just long enough to get it into the oil. And be super careful when frying the tomatoes – if the batter slips off, the moisture from the tomatoes will make the oil splatter.

Heat the oil in a deep-fryer or heavy-based saucepan to 170–180°C (340–350°F), or until a cube of bread dropped into the oil turns golden brown in 15–20 seconds.

In a bowl, combine the apple, cabbage, olive oil, vinegar, poppy seeds and 1 teaspoon of the salt. Add the black pepper and lemon juice to taste and mix well.

To make the fried tomatoes, combine the flour, soda water, cayenne pepper and mustard powder in a bowl. Whisk until smooth. Carefully put the cherry tomatoes into the mixture and spoon over the batter until well coated. Drain off the excess batter ever so slightly then fry the tomatoes for around 45–60 seconds, or until crisp and golden. Remove the tomatoes and drain them on a wire rack.

Lightly dust the tomatoes with the hot paprika and remaining salt, and serve with the apple slaw.

oil for deep-frying

1 **fuji apple** or other sweet red apple, cut into matchsticks

250 g (9 oz/3⅓ cups) shredded **green cabbage**

60 ml (2 fl oz/¼ cup) **olive oil**

60 ml (2 fl oz/¼ cup) **apple cider vinegar**

pinch of **poppy seeds**

1½ teaspoons **salt**

freshly ground **black pepper**

lemon juice to taste

35 g (1¼ oz/¼ cup) **self-raising flour**

80 ml (2½ fl oz/⅓ cup) **soda water (club soda)**

1 teaspoon **cayenne pepper**

½ teaspoon **mustard powder**

240 g (8½ oz) **cherry tomatoes** on the vine

1 teaspoon **hot paprika**

My favourite part of the chicken is the wing. The thing I like most is that you have to eat wings with your hands. This to me is one of the most pleasurable eating experiences there is. Yes, I'm serious – wings, wings and more wings!

These boss wings are hot, greasy and kinda fresh all at the same time. When we serve these in the truck, we throw a couple of tortillas in the bottom of the tray to help mop up the sauce.

BOSS WINGS WITH DANISH FETA AND CELERY LEAF

Serves **4**

Preheat the oven to 200°C (400°F).

Roast the chicken in a roasting tin for 25 minutes, or until the wings are a dark golden brown and the chicken is cooked through. Remove the wings from the oven and keep warm. Drain and reserve 60 ml (2 fl oz/¼ cup) of the roasting tin juices.

Heat the olive oil in a frying pan over medium heat. Fry the garlic until golden then add the chipotle chillies, adobo sauce, tomato sauce, reserved roasting tin juices and 60 ml (2 fl oz/¼ cup) water. Simmer for 2–3 minutes, or until the sauce thickens.

Add the chicken wings and stir to coat them in the sauce. Mix through half of the feta and half of the celery leaves and remove from the heat.

To serve, scatter over the remaining feta and celery leaves and add a pinch of sea salt to taste.

20 **chicken wings** (about 1 kg/2 lb 3 oz), tips removed, drumettes and wingettes separated

1 tablespoon **olive oil**

1 **garlic clove**, crushed

2 **chipotle en adobo**, chopped, plus 1 teaspoon adobo sauce (see page 21)

140 ml (4½ fl oz) **tomato sauce (ketchup)**

80 g (2¾ oz) **Danish feta**, crumbled

handful of **celery leaves**, chopped

sea salt to serve

CHILLI CHEESE CROQUETTES

Makes **7** croquettes

50 g (1¾ oz) **brie**

1 large **chipotle en adobo,**
plus 35 ml (1¼ fl oz)
adobo sauce (see page 21)

230 g (8 oz/1 cup) **mashed
potato** (colibans work well)

oil for deep-frying

35 g (1¼ oz/¼ cup)
plain (all-purpose) flour

1 **egg,** beaten

30 g (1 oz/½ cup)
**panko crumbs (Japanese
breadcrumbs)**

sliced pickled **jalapeños**
to serve (optional)

Cut the brie into 2 cm × 1 cm (¾ in × ½ in) chunks, or 7 equal-sized pieces. Cut the chipotle chilli into 1 cm (½ in) squares, or 7 equal-sized pieces. (You might like to make the chipotle pieces a bit smaller depending on how hot you like it.) Top each piece of brie with a piece of chipotle.

Scoop out a tablespoonful of mashed potato and roll it into a ball. Flatten it into a patty in your palm. Gently cup your hand to shape the potato so it resembles half a ping-pong ball. Put a piece of brie with chipotle into the centre and top with 1 teaspoon of the adobo sauce from the chilli. Gently and carefully work the potato around the filling until all the edges are completely sealed.

Preheat the oil in a deep-fryer or large heavy-based saucepan to 170°C (340°F), or until a cube of bread dropped into the oil turns golden brown in 20 seconds.

Prepare three small bowls – one with the flour, one with the egg and one with the panko crumbs. Roll each croquette in the flour, then the egg and then the breadcrumbs.

Shake off any excess crumbs and fry the croquettes for about 2 minutes, or until golden.

Serve with sliced pickled jalapeños on the side for an extra kick of heat.

oil for deep-frying

185 g (6½ oz/1¼ cups) **plain (all-purpose) flour**

½ teaspoon **cayenne pepper**

1 teaspoon **salt**

1 **egg**

350 g (12½ oz) raw **prawns (shrimp)**, shelled and deveined, roughly chopped

½ **red onion**, thinly sliced

handful of **coriander (cilantro) leaves**, chopped

brine from Pickled tomatoes (see pages 175–176) to serve

sour cream to serve

PRAWN NUGGETS

Makes *20* nuggets

My father was a super-resourceful cook. If you were hungry, he could pretty much make something happen out of nothing.

As kids, my brothers and I would always be poking around the kitchen on a Sunday afternoon, kinda hungry and kinda hopeless. It was too early for dinner, but we were still hungry. Mum would shout out, 'Eat an apple,' to which we would reply, 'But we're not hungry for that!'. 'Well, you can't be really hungry then,' my mum would say. At that point, my papa would always step in and whip up a lil' something. More times than not, it was little fried nuggets he called 'doodads'. If the cupboards were bare, the main ingredient would be onions and some dried prawns or ikan bilis.

I wanted to build on the nuggets by using some fresh prawns and coriander. It's very seldom that I deep-fry something and don't want a crispy exterior, but for these I really like a softer finish, which takes up the pickle juice much better. If you do want a crispy finish, then substitute the plain flour for self-raising flour and add 1 teaspoon of bicarbonate of soda (baking soda).

Heat the oil in a deep-fryer or large heavy-based saucepan over medium–low heat to 160–170°C (320–340°F), or until a cube of bread dropped into the oil turns golden brown in 20–25 seconds.

Meanwhile, whisk together the flour, cayenne pepper, salt, egg, prawns, onion, coriander and 250 ml (8½ fl oz/1 cup) water in a bowl until combined.

Scoop out a heaped tablespoonful of the mixture and gently drop it into the oil. Repeat with more of the mixture, without overcrowding the deep-fryer or saucepan. Fry for 3–4 minutes, or until golden brown, and drain on paper towel. Repeat until all of the batter is used up.

Serve with the pickled tomato brine and sour cream.

BASIL CHIPS

handful of **basil leaves**

sea salt

ANCHO SALT

1 **dried ancho chilli**
(see Recipe notes)

1 small **dried habañero
chilli** (see Recipe notes)

2 tablespoons **sea salt**

CHICKEN SKINS

sea salt

250 g (9 oz) **chicken skin**
(about 5 skins)
(see Recipe notes)

oil for deep-frying

CHICKEN RIBS

5 **chicken ribs** (about
150 g/5½ oz)

sea salt

lemon juice to taste

FRIED PICKLES

oil for deep-frying

50 g (1¾ oz/⅓ cup)
self-raising flour

80–125 ml (2½ fl oz–4 fl oz/
⅓ cup–½ cup) **soda water
(club soda)**

1 **gherkin (dill pickle)**,
sliced into 5 mm (¼ in)
rounds

BAR SNACKS:
BASIL CHIPS, CHICKEN SKINS, CHICKEN RIBS WITH ANCHO SALT, AND FRIED PICKLES

Serves *2* as a snack

If you're not a beer drinker, these go just fine with an ice-cold lemonade.

To make the basil chips, preheat the oven to 220°C (430°F). Pat the leaves dry if there is any moisture on them. Spread the leaves out on a baking tray lined with baking paper and lightly season with sea salt. Bake in the oven for 5 minutes, or until the leaves are crisp. Be careful not to burn them. Remove from the oven and let cool.

To make the ancho salt, heat a non-stick or cast-iron frying pan over a low–medium heat. Dry-toast the ancho chilli, turning frequently, or until the chilli is fragrant and pliable. Remove from the heat and cut out and discard the stem. Repeat the process with the dried habañero chilli. In a food processor or blender, blitz the chillies into a powder. Combine with the sea salt and mix well.

To make the chicken skins, lightly sprinkle salt over the them and let sit for 30 minutes. Wipe down the skins with paper towel to remove any moisture. Heat the oil in a small saucepan to 160°C (320°F), or until a cube of bread dropped into the oil turns golden brown in 25 seconds. Fry the chicken skins for about 5–7 minutes, or until crispy and golden brown. Drain on paper towel.

To make the chicken ribs, heat a chargrill pan over medium–high heat. Cook the chicken ribs, turning every minute or so, for 5–7 minutes, or until the ribs are nicely charred. Sprinkle with ancho salt and squeeze over some lemon juice to taste.

To make the fried pickles, heat the oil in a small saucepan over medium heat to 175–180°C (345–350°F), or until a cube of bread dropped into the oil turns golden brown in 15 seconds. Meanwhile, combine the flour and 80 ml (2½ fl oz/⅓ cup) of the soda water in a bowl to make a batter. If the batter is too thick, add more soda water – it should be the consistency of pouring (single/light) cream. Pick up each gherkin slice with a toothpick (this is the best way I know to get the pickle into the oil) and carefully coat it in the batter. Fry for 1 minute, or until crispy then drain on paper towel. Repeat with the remaining gherkin slices. Serve the beer snacks on a platter with American mustard, if desired.

Recipe notes: Dried ancho and habañero chillies: These can be purchased from South American food stores.

Chicken skins: Ask your butcher for these.

Bar Snacks: Basil Chips, Chicken Skin, Chicken Ribs with Ancho Salt and Fried Pickles

TOSTADAS

One of my first ever taco truck experiences in the States was at a seafood taco truck in East LA over by Highland Park. It was an old-school type of truck, no Twitter or Facebook, just the same spot day in and day out. I was staying with my good friend Jeff Jank from Stones Throw records. I had driven past this truck many a time between Jeff's office and his house but never thought to stop. Highland Park a few years ago didn't really have any spots for breakfast or lunch so I was always struggling to find something local. On one of these 'hungry in LA with no car' struggles, I walked on down to the truck and was really pleasantly surprised by the freshness of the seafood tostadas.

Tostadas are crisp-fried tortillas, and can be topped however you like – get creative. I love them; they make you think about what you're eating a little bit differently. Unlike a soft taco, which I always eat far too quickly, the tostada commands you to take your time, or the whole thing will come crashing down. Whenever we cater for a wedding or a party we always try and get the hosts to go with some tostadas for starters. I like to do a small tostada, which is around 5 cm (2 in) in diameter but you can easily go for bigger.

You can buy tostada chips from South American food stores. Otherwise, most supermarkets will carry plain, round corn (tortilla) chips, which work well as a substitute.

PRAWN TOSTADAS WITH SLAW AND TAMARIND SALSA

Makes *12* tostadas

12 **raw tiger prawns (shrimp)**, shelled and deveined, tails intact

oil for brushing

12 **tostada chips** (see page 52)

125 g (4½ oz/½ cup) **sour cream**

red cabbage, thinly sliced on a mandoline, to serve

small handful of **coriander (cilantro) leaves**, finely chopped

TAMARIND SALSA

10 g (¼ oz) finely chopped **chipotle en adobo** (see page 21)

10 g (¼ oz) **tamarind purée**

2 tablespoons **apple cider vinegar**

1 teaspoon **brown sugar**

Heat a frying pan or a barbecue hotplate to high. Lightly brush the prawns with oil and grill for 1–2 minutes on each side, or until just cooked through.

To make the tamarind salsa, whisk together all of the ingredients with 2 tablespoons water until combined.

To assemble, smear each tostada with 1½ teaspoons of the sour cream and top with a little cabbage, a prawn and 1 teaspoon of the tamarind salsa. Garnish with the coriander and serve.

SPICED SASHIMI TOSTADAS

Makes *12* tostadas

40 g (1½ oz/¼ cup) **sesame seeds**

1 tablespoon **light soy sauce**

½ teaspoon **mirin**

2 tablespoons **rice vinegar**

1 teaspoon **sesame oil**

1 teaspoon **brown sugar**

100 g (3½ oz) **sour cream** (see Recipe note)

300 g (10½ oz) **sashimi grade tuna,** finely diced

2 **radishes,** thinly sliced

favourite **hot sauce** to taste

12 **tostada chips** (see page 52)

lime juice to taste

small handful of **coriander (cilantro) leaves,** finely chopped

Toast the sesame seeds in a dry frying pan over low heat, shaking the pan occasionally, for 1–2 minutes or until lightly browned. Be careful not to burn them. Transfer to a mortar and use a pestle to grind into a rough powder.

In a food processor, pulse the sesame powder, soy sauce, mirin, rice vinegar, sesame oil and sugar until combined. Transfer to a small bowl and stir in the sour cream.

Combine the tuna with the radish and a splash of hot sauce in a bowl.

To assemble, spread each tostada with 1 teaspoon of the sesame sour cream mixture and top with some of the tuna mixture. Squeeze over some lime juice, scatter over the coriander and serve.

Recipe note: I like to use a thick organic sour cream.

1 quantity of the **black beans** from Potatoes and beans with cracked tortillas (pages 146–7)

12 **tostada chips** (see page 52)

crumbled **Danish feta** to serve

1 quantity **Quick pickled onions** (page 162), thinly sliced

finely chopped **coriander (cilantro) leaves** to serve

Use the black beans as cooked in Potatoes and beans with cracked tortillas (pages 146–7) for these tostadas.

BLACK BEAN TOSTADAS

Makes *12* tostadas

Prepare the black beans and allow to come to room temperature.

Scoop a tablespoonful of the beans onto each tostada and top with a little of the Danish feta, pickled onion slices and coriander.

This recipe uses chiltepil, a dry salsa made from sesame seeds, pepitas and chile de árbol. Use cold white beans from Verde meatballs and white beans (pages 148–9).

WHITE BEAN TOSTADAS

Makes *12* tostadas

1 **avocado,** thinly sliced

12 **tostada chips**
(see page 52)

½ quantity **White beans**
(see pages 148–149)

CHILTEPIL

70 g (2½ oz/½ cup) **pepitas (pumpkin seeds)**

40 g (1½ oz/¼ cup) **sesame seeds**

¼ teaspoon **salt**

½ teaspoon **sesame oil**

3–4 teaspoons **chilli flakes,** preferably chile de árbol (see page 21)

To make the chiltepil, toast the pepitas in a dry frying pan over low heat, until light brown and fragrant. Transfer to a mortar and use a pestle to break them up slightly.

Combine the pepitas with the sesame seeds, salt, sesame oil and chilli flakes.

To assemble, place 2 slices of avocado on each tostada and top with a spoonful of beans and a sprinkling of chiltepil.

CRACKERS

Every day after school was always hectic at our house. My father would come home around five and start working on dinner. At this point he would go into his own zone, and hated being asked what was on the menu. 'You get what I cook,' he would say. 'That's all well and good,' I would think, 'but what the hell do we eat now?'

I would generally rummage through the cupboards and pull out the crackers. With a bit of Vegemite and cheese, I was content for another hour. I have always taken crackers for granted. Kinda like breakfast cereal, I always just have them in the cupboard. This is probably the reason why I never thought to make them or spend any time on really nice toppings.

Now that my own kids are coming home ravenous every single day from school I am really thinking about what they eat before dinner. Too much and dinner will be a waste of time; too little and they lose it. So I either give them crackers or serve dinner at five!

I also love serving crackers as appetisers for dinner parties. If you don't have the time to make the crackers from scratch, plain lavash or other unleavened bread will do. Otherwise, these toppings also work well on tostadas.

½ teaspoon **dried yeast**

300 g (10½ oz/2 cups)
plain (all-purpose) flour,
sifted

80 ml (2½ fl oz/⅓ cup)
olive oil

1 teaspoon **salt**

sea salt to taste

CRACKERS

Makes *30* crackers

Dissolve the yeast in 2 tablespoons warm water. Using an
electric mixer or a food processor with a dough hook, mix
the yeast mixture with the flour until combined. Add 60 ml
(2 fl oz/¼ cup) of the oil and mix until incorporated. Dissolve
the salt in 100 ml (3½ fl oz) water and add it to the dough.
Mix on a low setting for 6–7 minutes, or until the dough is
smooth and even. Transfer the dough to a lightly oiled bowl,
cover with plastic wrap and set aside in a warm place for
about 1½ hours, or until the dough has doubled in size.

Preheat the oven to 200°C (400°F). Divide the dough into
4–5 equal-sized portions. Roll one portion of dough through
a pasta machine set to its widest setting, then repeat. Set
the pasta machine to a narrower setting, and roll the dough
through again. The dough should be about 1–2 mm (¹⁄₁₆–⅛ in)
thick. Lay the dough sheet on a lightly floured work surface.
Repeat the process with the remaining dough portions.

If you don't have a pasta machine, use a rolling pin to roll out
the dough until it is 1–2 mm (¹⁄₁₆–⅛ in) thick. Cut the dough
into 5 cm (2 in) squares. I like to use a fluted pastry wheel
to give the crackers a nice edge. Transfer to a baking tray lined
with baking paper. Combine the remaining oil with 1 tablespoon
water and lightly brush the squares with the mixture. Lightly
season with sea salt and bake for 10–15 minutes, or until the
crackers are lightly browned and crunchy.

I hated sardines as a kid – they were overly fishy and I hated the bones. My father would buy tinned sardines in tomato sauce. He would wash off the sauce and use the fish for stocks. I love sardines now and, lucky for me, the local market pretty much always has them.

SARDINE CRACKERS

Makes *12* double crackers

2 **rosemary** sprigs (about 20 cm/8 in long)

12 **sardine fillets**

olive oil for drizzling

sea salt

1 tablespoon **wholegrain (seeded) mustard**

20 g (¾ oz) **butter**

12 **double crackers** (5 cm × 10 cm/2 in × 4 in) (see Recipe note)

Thread 1 rosemary sprig through the top of each sardine fillet widthways, and a second rosemary sprig through the bottom of each fillet widthways, so that the sprigs are like skewers. Use the base of the rosemary as it will be the strongest.

Heat a chargrill pan or a barbecue to a medium–high heat.

Drizzle the fillets with a little bit of olive oil, just to stop them from sticking to the grill. Once the surface is nice and hot, cook the fillets for 1–2 minutes on each side, or until they are cooked through. Be careful when you flip them – you might want to use a spatula so the rosemary sprigs don't break.

Transfer the fillets to a plate and sprinkle with a pinch of sea salt. Set aside to cool slightly.

Meanwhile, use a fork to combine the mustard with the butter in a small bowl.

To serve, spread the mustard butter onto the crackers and top with the sardines.

Recipe note: You can either make your own crackers from scratch (see opposite) or use a plain lavash or other unleavened bread.

125 ml (4 fl oz/½ cup) **pineapple juice**

1 tablespoon **salt**

250 g (9 oz) **boneless, skinless chicken breast**

1 round fresh **pineapple** (about 10 cm/4 in wide × 2 cm/¾ in thick)

12 **double crackers** (5 cm × 10 cm/2 in × 4 in) (see Recipe notes)

butter to serve

60 ml (2 fl oz/¼ cup) **barbecue sauce** (see page 164)

Barbecue chicken pizza is pretty wrong – but I love it. In my early 20s, my crew and I did smash our fair share before heading out. Even as an adult, I still love the combination of grilled pineapple and barbecue sauce. Here's my twist.

CHICKEN CRACKERS

Makes *12* double crackers

In a non-metallic bowl, combine the pineapple juice, salt and 125 ml (4 fl oz/½ cup) water to make a brine. Add the chicken, cover and refrigerate overnight.

Heat a chargrill pan or barbecue (see Recipe notes) to a medium heat. Grill the pineapple for 3–4 minutes on each side, or until lightly charred. Transfer the pineapple to a chopping board and cut it into 12 pieces. Set aside.

Cook the chicken breast in the same chargrill pan or barbecue over medium heat for 5–6 minutes on each side, or until the chicken is cooked through. Transfer the chicken to a chopping board and let it cool slightly. Cut the chicken widthways into 1 cm (½ in) thick slices.

Simmer the barbecue sauce in a small saucepan for about 5 minutes, or until thickened.

To assemble, spread each cracker with a little butter and top with a slice of chicken, a teaspoon of the barbecue sauce and a piece of grilled pineapple.

Recipe notes: Crackers: You can either make your own crackers from scratch (page 62) or use plain lavash or other unleavened bread.

Barbecue: If you are using a barbecue with a hood, you can add some smoking chips to impart more depth of flavour into the chicken.

BEETROOT CRACKERS WITH FLUFFY CHEESE

Makes *12* double crackers

3 small **beetroot (beets)**, trimmed and unpeeled

2 **garlic cloves**, unpeeled

1 tablespoon **olive oil**

1 teaspoon **salt**

30 g (1 oz) **soft blue cheese**

30 g (1 oz) **cream cheese**

12 **double crackers** (5 cm × 10 cm/2 in x 4 in) (see Recipe note)

6 **cherry tomatoes**, halved

mint leaves to serve

Preheat the oven to 180°C (350°F).

Wrap the beetroot and garlic in a foil parcel and roast in the oven for 1 hour, or until the beetroot are cooked through.

Remove the beetroot and garlic from the oven and let cool. Peel the beetroot and cut them in half. Process the beetroot, garlic, olive oil and salt in a food processor until smooth, adding 1 tablespoon water while the motor is running to help loosen the mixture.

In a mixing bowl, use a whisk to smash together the blue cheese, cream cheese and 25 ml (1 fl oz) water until combined.

To assemble, spread a little beetroot mixture onto the crackers. Top with the cheese mixture and garnish with the cherry tomatoes and mint.

Recipe note: You can either make your own crackers from scratch (page 62) or use plain lavash or other unleavened bread.

TACOS

You always hear about people tasting an amazing dish for the first time and wanting to go back to that time or reproduce the experience. My first taco experiences were the opposite of that. I, like many other Australians, grew up only really knowing one type of taco – a hard-shell tortilla stuffed with packet-seasoned minced (ground) beef and topped with lettuce, tomato and cheese. My parents hated pre-packaged foods and seasonings but they would pick up a taco kit every now and again – an 'all-in-one' glossy box with a picture of a donkey and sombrero – to satisfy my brothers' and my appetite for the glamorous TV dinner lifestyle that the '80s so wholeheartedly endorsed. I would sit in front of the TV with my brothers on a Friday night, with an overloaded taco crumbling in my lap. At least we were playing Sega.

It wasn't until I travelled to the States in my 20s and started eating tacos from taco stands that I discovered what a real taco should taste like – simple, fresh, delicious – and I realised then that it all hinged on freshly made tortillas. From then on I became obsessed with the tortilla – both flour and corn – and began making my own.

But, it was a few years later that I got the chance to learn how to make tacos from a true master. I remember walking into a small supermarket in East LA and seeing that they were steeping dried corn to make masa. I got chatting to one of the staff about the process and I ended up grinding some corn and making fresh masa. Then the guy showing me the ropes said, 'My brother runs the taco store next door. Go in there and get him to cook these tortillas for you. Let him fill them with whatever he has left.'

I knocked on the door just as they were closing up. Armando, seeing the fresh ball of masa I was holding in my hand, shook his head with a warm grin and asked, 'My brother send you over here?'

'Yeah,' I said, 'but if you're all done, I understand.'

'Don't be silly,' he said. 'Take a seat.' I couldn't believe Armando's willingness to cook for me past closing time. He fixed me five small tacos. I was blown away. From the chicken tinga to the lengua, all were perfectly crafted. I had never had tacos this good. It turned out that I was sitting in Guisados, one of the best taco joints in LA.

Making tortillas from scratch is really what it's all about (see pages 26–27). It's the foundation of every great taco.

CRISPY PRAWN TACOS

Makes *8* tacos

If you don't have the time or the want to deep-fry these prawns, then by all means just grill them on your barbecue as they are, without the batter. They will be equally as good … well, maybe not equally but they will be pretty close.

FRESH CHILLI SALSA

3 **roma (plum) tomatoes**

1–2 **hot chillies,** or to taste

½ **white onion,** chopped

3 **garlic cloves**

2 teaspoons **salt**

juice of ½ **lime,** or to taste

SLAW

250 g (9 oz) **green cabbage** (about ¼ of a cabbage), thinly sliced on a mandoline

2 teaspoons **olive oil**

juice of ½ **lime**

small handful of **coriander (cilantro) leaves,** chopped

TEMPURA PRAWNS

250 ml (8½ fl oz/1 cup) iced **soda water (club soda)**

1 **egg**

100 g (3½ oz/⅔ cup) **self-raising flour**

1 teaspoon **cayenne pepper**

canola oil for deep-frying

16 raw **tiger prawns (shrimp)** (about 500 g/ 1 lb 2 oz), shelled and deveined, tails intact

8 **Corn tortillas** (pages 26–7)

whole egg mayonnaise to serve

chopped **coriander (cilantro) leaves** to serve

lime wedges to serve

To make the chilli salsa, bring a saucepan of water to the boil over a medium–high heat. Add the tomatoes and blanch for 30 seconds, then drain and transfer to a bowl filled with iced water. Peel and discard the skins.

Taste the fresh chilli to decide how much you want to use. As there are so many varieties, I always like to check the hotness on the tip of my tongue first. Remove and discard the stems. Combine the chillies with the tomatoes, onion, garlic, salt and 80 ml (2½ fl oz/⅓ cup) water in a food processor or blender. Process for about 30 seconds, or until smoothish, then strain. Season with a squeeze of lime juice. Transfer to a jar, seal and refrigerate for 4 hours, or overnight if you have the time.

To make the slaw, combine the cabbage, olive oil, lime juice and coriander in a bowl. Season with salt and mix well.

To make the tempura prawns, whisk together the soda water and the egg in a bowl until combined. Add the flour, cayenne pepper and a pinch of salt and whisk until the batter is the consistency of pouring (single/light) cream. If it's a little thin, add a touch more flour; if it's a little thick add a touch more iced soda water.

In a large heavy-based saucepan, heat the oil to 170–180°C (340–350°F), or until a cube of bread dropped into the oil turns golden brown in 15–20 seconds. Hold each prawn by the tail and dredge it through the batter, making sure it's well covered. Fry for about 2 minutes, or until the batter is golden brown. Remove the prawns and drain on paper towel.

To warm the tortillas, heat a non-stick frying pan over high heat. Warm the tortillas for about 10 seconds each, or until they become soft and pliable. If you are ready to construct the tacos, you can put them straight onto the serving plates; if not wrap them in a damp, clean tea towel (dish towel) to keep them soft.

To assemble, spread a little mayonnaise on each tortilla. Top with a little mound of the slaw, two crispy prawns and as much chilli salsa as you like. Garnish with coriander and the lime wedges.

200 ml (7 fl oz) **apple cider vinegar**

juice of 1 **lime,** or to taste

1 quantity **Flour tortillas** (page 27)

whole egg mayonnaise to serve

shredded **iceberg lettuce** to serve

quartered radishes to serve

lime wedges to serve

FROM SCRATCH

2 teaspoons **garlic powder**

1 teaspoon **brown sugar**

2 teaspoons **cayenne pepper**

2 teaspoons **smoked paprika**

1/2 teaspoon **ground coriander**

1 1/2 teaspoons **salt**

1.3 kg (2 lb 14 oz) whole **chicken,** butterflied

FROM THE CHICKEN SHOP

1 **barbecue chicken** (reserve the juice from the bag)

CHICKEN SHOP TACOS

Makes *20* tacos

I am going to take a guess and say that most families in Australia, at one point or another, have had a dinner consisting of a store-bought barbecue chicken, a loaf of white bread, iceberg lettuce, tomato and mayo. Growing up, this was on our table for dinner once every couple of weeks during the height of summer – mainly when my parents just couldn't be bothered cooking because of the heat. I remember the mad rush around the table, everyone grabbing the same few ingredients to slightly customise their sandwich. My mum would add chilli sauce, my brother pickles, and me, I would add avocado.

After moving out of home, I remember plonking the same ingredients on the table a few times. I am not sure whether it was the chicken, the hot summer or the absence of my brothers and my parents, but I could never recreate the mid-summer barbecue chicken dinner vibe with the same ingredients.

My fond childhood memories of my family tearing the charcoal chicken carcass to shreds seem unrepeatable – not even with my own family. My kids just have different tastes and my wife, Beci, hates white bread … but I just can't help tinkering with the dish ever so slightly to try to recreate that vibe all over again.

TOMATO SALSA

3 **roma (plum) tomatoes,** seeded and diced

1 **avocado,** stoned and diced

1 **gherkin (dill pickle),** finely chopped

1 tablespoon **olive oil**

juice of ½ **lime**

small handful of **croutons**

1 tablespoon finely chopped **red onion**

handful of **coriander (cilantro) leaves,** chopped

Preheat the oven to 160°C (320°F).

If cooking your own barbecue chicken, combine the garlic powder, sugar, cayenne pepper, smoked paprika, ground coriander and salt in a small bowl. Rub the spice mix all over the chicken, making sure it's well covered. Transfer the chicken to a small roasting tin. Add 125 ml (4 fl oz/½ cup) water to the tin and roast in the oven for 2½ hours. After the first hour, baste the chicken with the pan juices every 30 minutes. When the chicken is crispy and cooked through, remove it from the oven and let it rest.

To make the tomato salsa, combine all of the ingredients in a bowl and add salt to taste.

Shred the chicken meat from the bones and dress it with the apple cider vinegar and 2 tablespoons of the roasting tin juices or 2 tablespoons of juice from the chicken bag. Add a good pinch of salt, a squeeze of lime and chop it all together.

To warm the tortillas, heat a non-stick frying pan over high heat. Warm the tortillas for about 10 seconds each, or until they become soft and pliable.

To assemble, spread a small amount of whole egg mayonnaise on half of the tortilla, then top with some of the chicken, iceberg lettuce and tomato salsa. Serve with the radishes on the side and a fresh squeeze of lime.

BEEF SHORT RIB TACOS

My favourite thing about tacos is that they can be served crisp or soft, or somewhere in between. These beef tacos kinda fall in between – crispy but still a little bit chewy.

Makes **6** tacos

To prepare the salsa, preheat a woodfired oven, barbecue or regular oven to 180°C (350°F). Roast the tomatoes with the onion in a roasting tin for 1 hour, occasionally giving the tin a bit of a shake.

Use gloves to handle the habañero. Remove the stem and slice the chilli in half lengthways. If you like your salsa really hot, use the whole thing; if you prefer it more mild, just go for half or a quarter. Add the habañero to the roasting tin with the garlic and roast for another 30 minutes.

When the tomatoes are nice and soft with some charred spots, remove the roasting tin from the oven and let cool. Blitz the roasted vegetables in a food processor or with a hand-held blender until smooth. Strain the mixture into a bowl, using a wooden spoon to push it through a sieve. You will be left with a fair bit of pulp in the sieve – add a bit of pulp to the strained mixture, depending on how thick you like your salsa, and discard the rest of the pulp. Stir in the lime juice and vinegar to balance the flavour.

Prepare the ribs as per the method on page 162. Cut the meat from the bones and chop into 1–2 cm (½–¾ in) pieces.

To warm the tortillas, heat a non-stick frying pan over a high heat. Warm the tortillas for about 10 seconds each, or until they become soft and pliable.

To finish, heat the oil in a large non-stick frying pan or on a barbecue hot plate over a medium heat. Divide the beef between the tortillas, placing the beef on one half of each tortilla. Top with some of the provolone. Fold the tortillas in half and press down to form a semi-circular shape. Fry the filled tortillas for 1–2 minutes on each side, or until browned and crispy. Drain any excess oil and top with the salsa and coriander leaves.

1 quantity **ribs** from Ribs 'n' pickle (page 162)

6 **Corn tortillas** (pages 26–7)

125 ml (4 fl oz/½ cup) **olive oil**

60 g (2 oz) **provolone**, thinly sliced

chopped **coriander (cilantro) leaves** to serve

FIRE-ROASTED SALSA ROJA

1 kg (2 lb 3 oz) **roma (plum) tomatoes**, halved

1 **red onion**, quartered

1 **habañero chilli**

1 **garlic clove**, peeled

juice of 1 **lime**

1 tablespoon **white vinegar**

SWEETBREAD TACOS WITH CAULIFLOWER PURÉE AND HABAÑERO OIL

Makes **4** tacos

A few years back, I was lucky enough to be invited to the opening of an Argentinian restaurant in Sydney named Porteño. I was so taken by the big dramatic room with great décor and a large fire pit. Like at all good openings, whether it be an art show, a restaurant or a shop, the crowd's focus was on everything but the reason they were there – in this case, the food. My intention to eat a bunch of stuff didn't eventuate that night, not because there wasn't great food but because there were just too many people in the way for me to really check out the menu.

I returned a few months later to find the owners, Ben Milgate and Elvis Abrahanowicz, at the chopping boards that look out over the dining room. I was watching Ben chop some sweetbreads when, with the back of his knife, he pushed some my way. I was blown away; I had never tasted sweetbreads prepared like this before. Ever since, sweetbreads have been a staple at all of my barbecues. I just ask my butcher to put them aside for me.

1 tablespoon **salt**

250 g (9 oz) **sweetbreads** (preferably veal)

1 tablespoon **canola oil**

salt

4 **Corn tortillas** (pages 26–7)

lemon juice to serve

CAULIFLOWER PURÉE

300 g (10½ oz) **cauliflower** (about ¼ of a head), cut into florets

500 ml (17 fl oz/2 cups) **chicken stock**

¼ teaspoon **salt**

2 tablespoons **pouring (single/light) cream**

1 teaspoon **butter**

1 **garlic clove**, crushed

HABAÑERO OIL

2 **habañero chillies** (substitute dried if you can't find fresh)

125 ml (4 fl oz/½ cup) **olive oil**

To prepare the habañero oil, remove and discard the stems from the chillies and slice them in half lengthways. (Be sure to wear gloves while handling the chillies.) Heat a small saucepan over low heat and dry-fry the habañeros for 1–2 minutes, or until fragrant, being careful not to burn them. Pour in the olive oil and simmer gently for 30 minutes. Remove the habañero oil from the heat and let cool. Skim off any burnt seeds and transfer to a small sealable jar.

While the habañero oil is simmering, prepare the cauliflower purée. In a saucepan bring the chicken stock to the boil. Cook the cauliflower in the stock for 10 minutes, or until tender. Drain the cauliflower, reserving 125 ml (4 fl oz/½ cup) of the stock. In a food processor or blender, blitz the cauliflower, reserved liquid and all of the remaining ingredients until smooth. Set aside.

To prepare the sweetbreads, bring a small saucepan of water to the boil with the salt. Once boiling, reduce to a gentle simmer and add the sweetbreads. Cook for 15 minutes then drain and let cool. Wrap the sweetbreads in a clean tea towel (dish towel) and gently press out any excess liquid.

Heat the canola oil on a barbecue hotplate, in a chargrill pan or in a frying pan over a medium–high heat. Grill the sweetbreads for about 8–10 minutes on one side, and season with a good pinch of salt. Flip and grill on the other side, seasoning with more salt, and cook for another 8–10 minutes, or until nice and crispy.

Meanwhile, warm the tortillas. Heat a non-stick frying pan over high heat. Warm the tortillas for about 10 seconds each, or until they become soft and pliable. Wrap them in a damp, clean tea towel to keep them soft until ready to serve.

When the sweetbreads are ready, transfer them to a chopping board and slice them up. Give them a good squeeze of lemon and another pinch of salt.

To assemble, smear some of the cauliflower purée on each tortilla and top with slices of the sweetbreads. Drizzle over a little habañero oil and serve.

1 kg (2 lb 3 oz) **octopus tentacles**

olive oil for drizzling

6 **Corn tortillas** (pages 26–7)

lime wedges to serve

chopped **coriander (cilantro) leaves** to serve

SALSA

1 **guajillo chilli** (see Recipe note)

2 tablespoons **olive oil**, plus extra for drizzling

1 **red capsicum (bell pepper),** seeded and sliced

4 **garlic cloves,** crushed

2 teaspoons **ground cumin**

½ teaspoon **ground coriander**

60 ml (2 fl oz/¼ cup) **vinegar**

125 g (4½ oz/½ cup) **tinned tomatoes**

1 teaspoon **salt**

GRILLED OCTOPUS TACOS

Makes *6* tacos

The salsa in these tacos is somewhat inspired by shakshuka – that amazing Israeli dish of eggs baked in a rich tomato sauce. It is also great just with some corn (tortilla) chips. Be sure to leave it in the fridge overnight, or as long as you can, for the flavours to develop.

For the salsa, soak the guajillo chilli in a bowl of hot water for 30 minutes.

Meanwhile, heat the 2 tablespoons of olive oil in a saucepan over low heat. Cook the capsicum and garlic for 20 minutes, or until the capsicum is really soft. Stir in the ground cumin, ground coriander, vinegar, tinned tomatoes and salt.

Remove the guajillo chilli from the soaking liquid, reserving 80 ml (2½ fl oz/⅓ cup) of the liquid. Remove and discard the stem. Using a mortar and pestle, grind the chilli into a paste. Add the reserved soaking liquid, scrape down the sides of the mortar and work the liquid into the paste until well combined. Add the paste to the capsicum mixture and cook, covered, for 1 hour, still over low heat, stirring occasionally.

To prepare the octopus, bring a saucepan of water to the boil over medium heat. Cook the octopus for 45 minutes, or until nice and tender. Drain and refresh the octopus under cold water. Rub off the purple skin and pat dry with paper towel.

Preaheat a barbecue or chargrill pan to a high heat. Drizzle a little olive oil over the octopus and grill for 2–3 minutes per side, or until slightly charred. Remove from the heat and slice into chunks.

When the octopus is almost ready, warm the tortillas. If using a barbecue, warm the tortillas on the hotplate for about 10 seconds, or until they become soft and pliable. Alternatively, heat a non-stick frying pan over high heat and warm the tortillas for about 10 seconds each, or until soft and pliable. Wrap the tortillas in a damp, clean tea towel (dish towel) to keep them soft until ready to serve.

To assemble, spread a little of the salsa on a tortilla. As the salsa is quite sweet, you don't need much. Top with some of the octopus. Garnish with the lime wedges and some fresh coriander leaves and serve.

Recipe note: You can buy guajillo chillies from South American food stores.

TACO TRUCK POTATO TACOS

Makes *8* tacos

When I opened Beatbox Kitchen in 2009, I had dreams of opening for breakfast on Saturday mornings. I managed to get myself out twice! Both times were a struggle as getting everything packed after a late Friday night was hard. My breakfast idea was pretty simple: I'd have a steak sandwich and a potato taco on the menu. Most people who came ordered the taco. This is probably when I started thinking that I needed to have a second truck just for tacos.

The potato taco is probably my favourite out of all the tacos we make. My friend Jeff Jank first introduced me to the potato taco at El Atacor in LA. El Atacor is your regular low-key taqueria that's open late. After a couple of beers, their tacos de papa takes on a whole other dimension. I was so inspired that I started experimenting with my own potato taco. This is what we serve out of the Taco Truck.

2 **desiree or other all-purpose potatoes,** sliced 5 mm (¼ in) thick

250 g (9 oz/1 cup) **ricotta**

10 g (⅓ oz) sliced pickled **jalapeños,** roughly chopped

250 g (9 oz) **red cabbage** (about ¼ of a cabbage), thinly sliced on a mandoline

1 tablespoon **red wine vinegar**

salt

8 **Corn tortillas** (pages 26–7)

190 ml (6½ fl oz/¾ cup) **canola oil** (see Recipe note)

SALSA VERDE

½ small **white onion,** roughly chopped

handful of **coriander (cilantro) leaves and stems,** chopped

juice of 1 **lime**

1 **garlic clove**

1–2 fresh or pickled **jalapeños**

2 fresh or pickled **tomatillos,** chopped

pinch of **salt**

Bring a small saucepan of water to the boil. Cook the potato slices for about 10 minutes, or until cooked through, then drain.

Mix together the ricotta and the sliced pickled jalapeños in a bowl.

In another bowl combine the red cabbage with the red wine vinegar and a pinch of salt.

To make the salsa verde, combine all of the ingredients in a food processor or blender and blitz until smoothish.

Heat a non-stick frying pan over high heat. Warm the tortillas for about 10 seconds each, or until they become soft and pliable. Arrange the cooked potato slices on one half of each tortilla. Sprinkle with a pinch of salt and fold over.

Heat the canola oil in a frying pan over medium heat. Fry the tacos for 2–3 minutes on one side, then flip carefully and fry on the other side for 2–3 minutes, or until crispy. Drain the tacos on paper towel. To serve, spread some of the jalapeño ricotta over each taco. Top with some red cabbage and salsa verde.

Recipe note: You may need slightly more or less oil to fry the tacos. The oil in the pan needs to be 5 mm (¼ in) deep.

LAMB TACOS WITH ROCKET, POMEGRANATE CREMA AND CHILTEPIL

Makes **20** tacos

I am very fortunate to have two great brothers, Rudin and Johann. Both, like me, share a passion for food and family. Rudin has a beautiful little boy named Zedrin. For Zeddy's first birthday, Rudin decided to throw a big party, as you do. He invited about 100 people to his house and got me to sort out some food. As the guests started to arrive, they could see that Rudin and Brooke had gone to A LOT of effort for a first birthday party. They had custom badges and bunting made with Zeddy's name on them, plus there were endless drinks and snacks on offer. There was a buzz in the air, but no one could really pinpoint why. Sure, first birthdays are exciting, but this was out of the ordinary.

I had a spit of lamb shoulders going and, at about 1 pm, I was looking to start serving lunch. 1 pm came and Rudin gave me the nod. He and Brooke slipped back into the house. Five minutes later they re-appeared in new outfits and announced they were going to get married, then and there! A strange guest who had been posing as a distant relative popped out of the crowd and started the ceremony. WTF! Still in shock, all of the guests witnessed a very casual, but incredible, backyard wedding. Then they turned around and hit these spit-roasted lamb tacos!

Now, every time I make these tacos, I think of my brother's surprise wedding.

2 teaspoons **dried oregano**

2 teaspoons **hot paprika**

2 teaspoons **salt**

2 kg (4 lb 6 oz) **lamb shoulder,** bone removed

20 **Corn tortillas** (pages 26–7)

juice of 1 **lemon,** plus more to taste

rocket (arugula) to serve

chiltepil to taste, (page 57)

pomegranate seeds to serve

LABNEH

500 g (1 lb 2 oz/2 cups) **Greek-style yoghurt**

½ teaspoon **salt**

To make the labneh, combine the yoghurt with the salt in a bowl. Lay a large square of muslin (cheesecloth) on a working surface and scoop the yoghurt into the centre. Gather up the sides of the muslin to make a pouch around the yoghurt and tie up with kitchen string. Hang the pouch over a bowl and refrigerate for at least 24 hours (see Recipe note).

Preheat the oven to 140°C (275°F).

Combine the oregano, paprika and salt in a small bowl. Rub the spice mix all over the lamb and put the lamb, fat side up, in a roasting tin. Loosely cover the tin with foil and roast in the oven for 5 hours, or until the lamb is really tender and falling apart. Remove the lamb from the tin and let it rest for 15 minutes.

Heat a barbecue or a chargrill pan to a high heat. Cut the lamb into small pieces, and put aside any pieces with a good amount of fat. Cover the leaner lamb pieces with foil to keep them warm, and quickly grill the fatty pieces on the barbecue or in the chargrill pan for 2–3 minutes. Be sure to let some of the pieces really crisp up, and even burn slightly.

Meanwhile, warm the tortillas. Heat a non-stick frying pan or a barbecue hot plate to a high heat. Warm the tortillas for about 10 seconds each, or until they become soft and pliable. Wrap them in a damp, clean tea towel (dish towel) to keep them soft until ready to serve.

Combine the charred lamb with the rest of the lamb and hit it with a good squeeze of lemon and a good pinch of salt. To assemble, spread some of the labneh on each tortilla and top with some of the rocket, some of the lamb and a little chiltepil. Garnish with pomegranate seeds and serve.

Recipe note: The easiest way to hang the pouch is to tie it to a wooden spoon and suspend that over the bowl.

SOFT SHELL CRAB TACOS WITH JALAPEÑO VINAIGRETTE

Makes **4** tacos

Crabs and tortillas (when folded) share the same shape, so in my mind they are a natural fit.

To make the jalapeño vinaigrette, whisk together all of the ingredients in a bowl until combined. Set aside.

Heat the canola oil in a frying pan over high heat.

Combine the flour with the cayenne pepper and salt in a bowl. Lightly coat the crabs in the flour mixture and fry for 1–2 minutes on each side, or more depending on the size of the crabs. The crabs will turn pinkish when ready. Drain on paper towel.

Meanwhile, warm the tortillas. Heat a non-stick frying pan over high heat. Warm the tortillas for about 10 seconds each, or until they become soft and pliable.

To assemble, lightly spread each tortilla with a little mayonnaise and add a few strands of the cabbage and some of the coriander. Top with a crab and spoon over the jalapeño vinaigrette.

Recipe note: Put the crabs in the freezer for about 30 minutes before you want to clean them. Use scissors to cut across the top of the crab to remove the face and eyes. Lift up the flap on the left- and right-hand sides of the crab and remove the spongy lungs. Flip over the crab and cut out the flap on the underside.

60 ml (2 fl oz/¼ cup) **canola oil**

50 g (1¾ oz/⅓ cup) **plain (all-purpose) flour**

2 teaspoons **cayenne pepper**

pinch of **salt**

4 **soft shell crabs**, cleaned (see Recipe note)

4 **Corn tortillas** (pages 26–7)

whole egg mayonnaise to serve

green shredded **cabbage** to serve

chopped **coriander (cilantro) leaves** to serve

JALAPEÑO VINAIGRETTE

60 ml (2 fl oz/¼ cup) **olive oil**

1 tablespoon **white vinegar**

1 **jalapeño**, finely chopped

½ teaspoon **dijon mustard**

CONFIT DUCK TACOS WITH NECTARINE SALSA

Makes **4** tacos

5 **garlic cloves**

1 tablespoon **salt**

2 **duck legs** (about 500 g/ 1 lb 2 oz)

1 tablespoon **duck fat**

sea salt to taste

4 **Corn tortillas** (pages 26–7)

½ quantity **guacamole** (see pages 34–5)

NECTARINE SALSA

1 **white nectarine,** diced

1 **yellow nectarine,** diced

small handful of **coriander (cilantro) leaves,** finely chopped

¼ **white onion,** finely diced

juice of ¼ **lime**

In a small saucepan, combine 1 litre (34 fl oz/4 cups) water with the garlic and salt to make a brine. Warm over medium heat until the salt dissolves, then transfer the liquid to a bowl and set aside to cool. Add the duck legs to the cooled brine. Cover and refrigerate overnight.

The next day, remove the duck legs from the brine and pat them dry with paper towel. Pierce the legs in several places with a sharp skewer. Try to pierce into the underlying fat without piercing into the flesh. This will help the fat escape from under the skin so the skin will become crispy.

Put the duck fat into a small roasting tin. Add the duck legs and roast in the oven at 170°C (340°F) (without preheating) for 2 hours, or until the meat is tender and the skin is really crispy.

To make the nectarine salsa, combine all of the ingredients in a bowl.

When the duck legs are ready, remove them from the oven and let them rest for a few minutes.

Meanwhile, warm the tortillas. Heat a non-stick frying pan over high heat. Warm the tortillas for about 10 seconds each, or until they become soft and pliable.

With a sharp knife gently remove the crispy skin from the duck legs. Cut each piece of skin into 3 equal-sized pieces. Shred the meat from the bones. In a bowl, combine the shredded meat with 2–3 tablespoons of the roasting tin juices and a good pinch of sea salt.

Spread some of the guacamole onto each tortilla. Add a little confit duck and some of the salsa then top with the crispy skin.

FRIED CHICKEN TACOS WITH SPICED EGGPLANT

Makes *8* tacos

To make the spiced eggplant, grill the eggplant on a gas stove or barbecue, directly over a medium flame. Cook the eggplant, using tongs to turn it every minute, for 20–25 minutes, or until the flesh is really soft and the skin has blackened.

Let the eggplant cool then slice it in half lengthways. Gently scoop out all of the flesh and transfer to a colander to drain for 15 minutes. Discard the skin.

Roughly chop the eggplant and combine it with 60 ml (2 fl oz/¼ cup) water and all of the remaining spiced eggplant ingredients in a bowl. Mix well.

To make the fried chicken, heat the oil in a frying pan to 170°C (340°F), or until a cube of bread dropped into the oil turns golden brown in 20 seconds.

Coat the chicken strips in the potato flour. Shake off any excess flour then fry the chicken for 5–6 minutes, or until crispy and golden brown. Drain the chicken on paper towel and sprinkle with sea salt to taste.

Meanwhile, warm the tortillas. Heat a non-stick frying pan over high heat. Warm the tortillas for about 10 seconds each, or until they become soft and pliable.

To assemble, top each tortilla with the spiced eggplant and the fried chicken. Scatter over some coriander and serve with the lime wedges and extra chilli flakes, if liked.

Recipe note: The oil in the pan needs to be 5 mm (¼ in) deep.

8 **Corn tortillas** (see pages 26–7)

coriander (cilantro) leaves to serve

lime wedges to serve

SPICED EGGPLANT

1 **eggplant (aubergine)**, unpeeled

1 teaspoon **pomegranate molasses**

2 tablespoons **tahini**

1 **garlic clove**, crushed

1 tablespoon **lemon juice**

handful of **coriander (cilantro) leaves**, chopped

½–1 tablespoon **chilli flakes** (depending on how hot you like it), plus extra to serve

FRIED CHICKEN

canola or peanut oil for shallow-frying (see Recipe note)

800 g (1 lb 12 oz) **boneless, skinless chicken thighs**, cut into large strips

150 g (5½ oz/1 cup) **potato flour**

sea salt

BLACKENED SALMON TACOS WITH MINT CREMA AND CHICHARRÓN

Makes **4** tacos

Chicharrón is the term for crispy pig skin that has been stewed down and deep-fried, but it can apply to fish, too. I have always loved getting the skin on salmon nice and crispy, but sometimes I overcook the fish. With this method you can get both exactly how you like them.

1 tablespoon **salt**

500 g (1 lb 2 oz) **salmon fillet**, skin left on

grapeseed oil for deep-frying

25 g (1 oz) **butter**, melted

4 **Corn tortillas** (pages 26–7)

100 g (3½ oz) shredded red cabbage

SPICE RUB

1 teaspoon **smoked paprika**

2 teaspoons **brown sugar**

½ teaspoon **ground cumin**

½ teaspoon **garlic powder**

½ teaspoon **cayenne pepper**

½ teaspoon **salt**

½ teaspoon **black pepper**

1 teaspoon **dried thyme**

1 teaspoon **dried oregano**

½ teaspoon **allspice**

MINT CREMA

60 g (2 oz/¼ cup) **plain yoghurt**

60 g (2 oz/¼ cup) **whole egg mayonnaise**

pinch of **salt**

freshly ground **black pepper**

15 g (½ oz/¼ cup) chopped **mint leaves**

15 g (½ oz) chopped **spring onions (scallions)**

juice of ¼ **lime**

Preheat the oven to 70°C (160°F).

To make the fish chicharrón, combine the salt and 1 litre (34 fl oz/4 cups) water in a saucepan and bring it to the boil. With a very sharp knife, carefully remove the skin from the salmon fillet. Cook the skin in the boiling water for 3–4 minutes. Remove, and lay it out flat on paper towel to drain. Once it has cooled down, gently scrape off any excess meat with a butter knife and discard. Pat dry any moisture then cut the skin into 4 equal-sized pieces. Transfer to a baking tray lined with baking paper and bake in the oven for 1½ hours (see Recipe note).

Meanwhile, make the mint crema. Combine all of the ingredients in a bowl and mix well.

To finish the fish chicharrón, heat the oil in a small heavy-based saucepan to 180°C (350°F), or until a cube of bread dropped into the oil turns golden brown in 15 seconds. Fry the dried skins until crispy, usually around 15–25 seconds. Remove the skins with a slotted spoon and season straight away with a pinch of sea salt. Set aside.

Heat a cast-iron or heavy-based frying pan over high heat for 10–15 minutes so the surface is very hot.

Meanwhile, mix together all of the spice rub ingredients. Cut the salmon into 4 equal-sized portions. Dip the salmon pieces in the melted butter then coat them with the spice rub.

Cook the salmon in the searing hot pan for 1–2 minutes, or until a black crust forms. Flip the salmon, being sure to scrape all of the crust, too, and cook on the other side for another 1–2 minutes, or until blackened.

Warm the tortillas in a non-stick frying pan over high heat for about 10 seconds each, or until they become soft and pliable.

Scatter some red cabbage over each tortilla and top with a piece of blackened fish. Spoon over the mint crema and top with the fish chicharrón.

Recipe note: If it's a hot day, you can dry the salmon skins in the sun for a few hours instead of using the oven.

In a bowl, combine the sweet potato with the paprika and cumin until well coated. Heat two-thirds of the olive oil in a heavy-based saucepan over low–medium heat. Gently fry the sweet potato for 10 minutes, or until tender and starting to caramelise.

Meanwhile, make the cracked quinoa. Heat the olive oil in a non-stick frying pan and fry the quinoa over medium heat for 3–4 minutes, or until crunchy. Set aside to cool.

When the sweet potato is cooked, remove three-quarters to a bowl and set aside. Add the remaining olive oil and the crushed garlic to the pan and gently cook for 2 minutes. Add the beans and the stock, cover and simmer for 5 minutes.

Meanwhile, make a crema by combining the yoghurt with 1 tablespoon water.

Remove the lid from the pan and cook the bean mixture for another 2 minutes, or until it has thickened slightly.

Warm the tortillas in a non-stick frying pan over a high heat for about 10 seconds each, or until they become soft and pliable.

Spoon the bean mixture onto the warmed tortillas and top with the spiced sweet potato, the crema, the cracked quinoa, red onion and parmesan, if using. Finish with a fresh squeeze of lime.

150 g (5½ oz) **sweet potato,** cut into 1 cm (½ in) cubes

1 teaspoon **hot paprika**

½ teaspoon **ground cumin**

60 ml (2 fl oz/¼ cup) **olive oil**

4 **garlic cloves,** crushed

400 g (14 oz) tinned **black beans,** drained

125 ml (4 fl oz/½ cup) **chicken or vegetable stock**

60 g (2 oz/¼ cup) **plain yoghurt**

4 **Corn tortillas** (see pages 26–7)

thinly sliced **red onion** to serve

grated parmesan to serve (optional)

lime wedges for squeezing over

CRACKED QUINOA

1 teaspoon **olive oil**

50 g (1¾ oz) cooked **quinoa**

BEAN TACOS WITH SWEET POTATOES AND CRACKED QUINOA

Makes **4** tacos

BURGERS
& SANDWICHES

I used to be a bit scared of the multi-day music festival for two reasons. The first being that growing up listening to rap music meant that I was quite concerned with staying fresh. From T-shirts to sneakers, the idea of dirt and camping was a bit hard to deal with. But the kitchen is a humbling place – there's no room for ego. I quickly got over it and got the job done. The second reason was that I was really worried I wouldn't be able to eat well. To many, the food at a festival is secondary to the music, but I feel the balance is really starting to change and better food just enhances the whole festival experience.

When we first started doing a few festivals here and there, I usually just brought along some extra ingredients for staff meals. Nowadays, there are lots more great food stands as festival promoters are starting to understand the importance of having a good selection of food. I have always thought the best things to eat were burgers and sandwiches. No time for cutlery when you're running to catch a band.

Here are some of my favourite burgers and sandwiches.

BURGERS

Burgers really are one of those foods with different meanings for most people, which is why I don't like media things like 'Top 10 burgers'. Burgers are a comfort food and evoke a lot of memories for people. That's why people get so passionate about having or not having their favourite burger rated in reviews.

Since I can remember, eating burgers has become its own event in my mind – the burger itself was rarely as memorable as the company I was with or the fun I was having at the time. When I was 11, my mum would take us to McDonald's on a Friday night. When I was 15, I would walk and meet friends at the local fish and chip shop for a burger. When I was 20, I would have barbecue burgers for all my skate crew. I loved these times and the burger event has outdone the burger itself in many ways. Sure the Happy Meal is not the best around, but you can't replace the fun my brothers and I had tearing around the indoor play centre, or the independence that I felt ordering with my friends at the local fish and chip shop, or the laughs I had with my crew at our barbecues.

It wasn't until I started travelling through the States at age 25 that I discovered how awesome a burger could really be. I travelled all over the country, from the east to the west coast, eating all sorts of burgers. It didn't matter whether I was in New York, LA, San Fran', Detroit or San Diego, great burgers always had two things in common – simplicity and attention to detail. Along the way I met some amazing, hardworking people running small diners whose commitment to the burger honestly inspired me.

Once I understood the fundamentals of what I believed made a great burger, I wanted to share it with others, which is why I started Beatbox Kitchen. Beatbox to me is way more than the burger; it's about community and creating a space where fond memories and distinct neighbourhood moments can form.

My idea of a great burger is something that doesn't take too long to prepare, is enjoyed with friends and oozes juice. Here are some of my ideas regarding burgers. Please see what works for you.

MY PERFECT BURGER

I like to keep my patty in proportion to my bread. I hate a bad bread-to-beef ratio, which is why I work backwards from the bread.

Measure your bread roll then press out your patties to be at least 10–15 per cent bigger in circumference, as they will shrink.

Cuts like chuck and brisket with an 80/20 meat to fat ratio work well. Get your butcher to prepare the minced (ground) meat with this ratio.

Treat your patty with the same respect you would show a fine steak.

For me the beef needs to be the star; any other topping that is obstructing rather than enhancing the beef needs to go. This is what I build from. I want the cheese to be creamy and mellow, the lettuce to give a little snap and the tomato to refresh.

The onion just helps balance the beef and the mayo. Hot sauce and mustard are there to add some extra spice and sour. Careful though; it's easy to go overboard.

COOKING A GREAT PATTY

Heat a barbecue, chargrill pan or frying pan over a high heat.

Season the patty with salt and cook salt side down. Give it a little extra salt while it's cooking. Flip when a crust has formed and when the sides have also cooked about halfway up, and then add cheese. I like to cook my burgers to medium-rare, which is around 2–3 minutes each side depending on the weight of the patty. Give your patty a minute to rest.

THE MAYO

The mayo can make or break a burger. I do like a tangy mayo with my burger, which I've included below. It's a good base and if you like it a bit sweeter you can add some tomato sauce. Happy slathering!

STRAIGHT MAYO

In a bowl, whisk together the egg yolks, mustard and 1 teaspoon of the salt until combined. Continue to whisk and slowly drizzle in the oil. Give yourself a break every 50 ml (1¾ fl oz) and add in 1 teaspoon of the lemon juice. Keep going until all the oil and lemon juice has been used.

2 **egg yolks**

1 teaspoon **dijon mustard**

2 teaspoons **salt**

300 ml (10 fl oz) **grapeseed oil**

1 tablespoon **lemon juice**

TANGY MAYO

Stir the cayenne pepper and pickle through the straight mayo until well combined.

1 teaspoon **cayenne pepper**

1 **gherkin (dill pickle),** roughly chopped

1 quantity **Straight mayo** (see above)

150 g (5½ oz) **minced (ground) beef skirt (flank) steak**

150 g (5½ oz) **minced (ground) beef short rib** (see Recipe note)

2 tablespoons **olive oil**

1 **brown onion,** sliced

1 **tinned chipotle en adobo,** chopped, plus 2 tablespoons **adobo sauce** (see page 21)

1 **dried habañero chilli**

sea salt

2 **eggs**

2 **burger buns**

butter to serve

shredded white cabbage to serve

TT × BBK BURGER

Makes **2** burgers

I did this burger a few years ago with my friend Dave Kerr, a quality barman who runs an awesome mariner-style pub in inner Melbourne. He gave me a call and said he wanted a burger to go with a michelada he was putting together for an article about burgers and drinks. A michelada is a Mexican cocktail made with beer, lime juice, spices and vegie juice or clamato – a blend of clam juice and tomato juice. Like a michelada, this burger is great for a hangover.

Mix together the minced skirt steak and the minced short rib in a bowl. Try not to overwork the meat.

Heat 1 tablespoon of the olive oil in a frying pan over a low heat. Gently sauté the onion for 2–3 minutes, or until softened. Stir in the chipotle and the adobo sauce and cook for 10 minutes then remove to a bowl and set aside.

Meanwhile, in a small non-stick frying pan over a low heat, dry-fry the habañero, turning it frequently so it doesn't burn, for 2–3 minutes, or until fragrant and softened slightly. Transfer to a chopping board and let cool. Finely chop the habañero into flakes. (I suggest you use gloves. These chillies are no joke.)

Bring a heavy-based frying pan to a medium heat. Divide the minced meat mixture into 2 portions. Work each portion into a patty about 1 cm (½ in) thick and season with sea salt. Cook the patties the same way you like your steak. I like mine medium–rare, so I cook them for 2 minutes on each side. After flipping the patties, add the chipotle onions to the pan and cook for about 1 minute. When the patties are cooked to your liking, remove them from the pan along with the chipotle onions. Let the patties rest for 1–2 minutes.

Heat the remaining olive oil in the same frying pan over a low heat. Add a pinch (or more if you like it hot) of the habañero chilli flakes and cook for 30 seconds. Crack the eggs into the pan, on top of the chilli flakes, and fry until the whites have set. Remove the eggs from the pan and drain.

Lightly toast the buns under the grill (broiler).

To build the burgers, butter the buns and add some shredded cabbage. Top with a patty, a fried egg and the onions.

Recipe note: Ask your butcher to prepare the short rib mince for you.

TT x BBK Burger

Delicious

SHROOM BURGER

Makes **4** burgers

In the early '90s, one of the first alternative shopping streets in Melbourne was Greville Street in a suburb called Prahran. The street was all of about 200 metres (220 yards) long and had a great skate store, a record store, clothes shops and a live music venue. There was also a small park and, on Sundays, they held a market. I wasn't much into vintage clothes and trinkets, but I was into the vegie burger stand run by a guy called Jerry. He set up his stand every Sunday, made an amazing patty of lentils and potato, grilled it and topped it with fresh salad. I was 16 at the time, and too shy to tell Jerry how much I loved his burger. Twenty years later, I got the chance to tell him when we met at an event. We now do a handful of events together and I am constantly inspired by him and his commitment to his burger. In honour of Jerry, here's my vegie burger.

2 tablespoons **olive oil**

4 **thyme sprigs**

4 large **portobello mushrooms,** stalks removed

4 slices **gouda**

4 **burger buns**

1 quantity **Tangy mayo** (page 105)

4 **baby cos (romaine) lettuce leaves**

2 **tomatoes,** sliced

½ **red onion,** thinly sliced

Combine the olive oil, thyme and mushrooms in a bowl. Cover and let marinate for a couple of hours.

Heat a non-stick frying pan over low–medium heat. Cook the mushrooms, stalk side down, for 4–5 minutes, or until the gills start to glisten. Add a slice of gouda and cook for a further 1–2 minutes, or until the cheese has melted.

Meanwhile, lightly toast the burger buns under a hot grill (broiler). To assemble, spread some tangy mayo on each bun and top with one of the mushrooms. Add lettuce, tomato and onion and serve.

Melbourne is geographically divided by the Yarra River, which gives a north and south to the city. I grew up in Frankston, which was one hour south of Melbourne and I never paid the divide any mind until I started to catch some pro-northside sentiments around the end of the '90s. As time went on, I moved closer to the city but always stayed southside. Not sure why – I would sometimes hear myself saying stupid things like, 'I just need to be near the beach,' (even though I never went there when I was growing up), and my favourite, 'There are just more trees in the south.' The truth was the north was unknown to me and I was a bit scared.

A few friends had moved to Brunswick, an eclectic northside suburb with a strong Middle Eastern vibe. I visited a couple of times and began to love the kebab delights of the area, but I still preferred the leafy tree-lined streets of the southside suburbs. The problem was, southside rentals near the city were super expensive. Beci and I needed to move house and she suggested we check out a place in West Brunswick. I begrudgingly went along. I liked it but I had reservations.

LA PALOMA SANDWICH: PASTRAMI AND BASIL PICKLES

Makes *8* sandwiches

One day, I went to Brunswick by myself and went for a little walk to see what I could find. I stumbled upon a tiny café just off Sydney Road, the main street in Brunswick, named La Paloma. There was no apparent menu – just a coffee machine, a turntable and soccer memorabilia. I asked the owner, who was called Todd, what he had for lunch. He replied, 'We make one roll here. Would you like that?' I was kinda shocked and excited at the same time. I said, 'Yes I would.' The La Paloma roll came with lettuce, mayo, avo, tomato, cucumber, Turkish pastirma (kinda like pastrami) and basil. I started eating it. I had to pause for a brief second while I was struck by an epiphany. This roll was everything I had ever wanted – delicious, simple, fresh, low-key and served by a very honest person. This roll represented Brunswick, or everything that I wanted from an area I could call home. After that moment, I pulled out all the stops to make sure we moved to Brunswick. We've lived there ever since.

Pastirma is more like a spicy bresaola than traditional pastrami. I really love the saltiness of the beef combined with the cucumber and the basil. Here is my ode to the La Paloma roll. You'll need to begin preparing the pastrami five to six days before you want to eat this sandwich. You'll also need a barbecue with a lid to trap the smoke and a thermometer so you can watch the temperature when smoking the brisket.

1 **loaf rye bread**

QUICK BASIL PICKLES

10 **peppercorns**

1 **garlic clove**, crushed

2 **basil stalks**

250 ml (8½ fl oz/1 cup) **white vinegar**

3 teaspoons **salt**

600 g (1 lb 5 oz) **pickling cucumbers** or **Lebanese (short) cucumbers**

PASTRAMI (See Recipe notes)

1 cup (300 g/10½ oz) **kosher (coarse) salt**

1 teaspoon **pink curing salt** (optional)

1 tablespoon **garlic powder**

95 g (3¼ oz/½ cup) **brown sugar**

1 tablespoon **mustard powder**

80 g (2¾ oz) **black peppercorns**

1 x 2 kg (4 lb 6 oz) **brisket** with deckle left on

60 g (2 oz) **coriander seeds**

180 g (6 oz/2 cups) **smoking woodchips**, soaked for 1 hour

To make the quick basil pickles, combine all of the ingredients, except the cucumbers, with 250 ml (8½ fl oz/ 1 cup) water in a large, sterilised, sealable jar. Stir until the salt has dissolved then add the cucumbers and firmly seal the jar. Refrigerate overnight or for at least 2 days for best results (see Recipe notes).

To make the pastrami, combine the kosher salt, pink curing salt, if using, garlic powder, brown sugar, mustard powder and 1 tablespoon of the black peppercorns with 4 litres (136 fl oz/16 cups) water in a large stockpot. Bring to the boil over a high heat. Once the salt and sugar have dissolved, remove the pot from the heat and let the liquid cool completely. Put the brisket in a large, sealable container then pour over the cooled brine, making sure the brisket is completely submerged. Use a plate to weigh it down if necessary. Seal the container and refrigerate for 4–6 days to let the brine penetrate. (See Recipe notes.)

Soak the brisket in cold water for at least 10–20 minutes, changing the water every 5 minutes to remove any excess salt. Grind the remaining peppercorns and coriander seeds using a mortar and pestle and apply liberally all over the brisket.

To smoke the brisket, preheat a barbecue for direct cooking over a low heat (see Recipe notes).

Once the barbecue temperature has stabilised to 100–110°C (210–230°F), put the brisket in. Put the woodchips in a disposable aluminium roasting tin on the grill plate of the barbecue. Smoke the brisket, with the lid closed, for about 2 hours, making sure the temperature stays around 110–120°C. Continue cooking after the smoke has cleared for another 4 hours, or until the internal temperature of the brisket is 85°C (185°F).

Transfer the brisket to a steamer over a saucepan of boiling water. Steam the brisket, covered, for 1½–2 hours. (If you are feeding a big crew, then go ahead and steam the whole brisket. If you only want some for a sandwich, then portion off what you need and put the rest in the fridge – 500 g (1 lb 2 oz) of brisket will need to be steamed for an hour.)

Remove the brisket from the steamer and slice it against the grain. Serve the brisket in the bread rolls with some sliced basil pickles.

Recipe notes: Pastrami: If you don't have the time or the space to brine a brisket, you can have your butcher prepare a brisket in the same way they would a corned beef. Then you can go straight to the smoking stage.

Pickles: The left-over quick basil pickles will keep in the fridge for 5-6 days.

Brining: You can use a meat injector, if you have one, to insert the brine directly into the brisket and speed up the brining process. If you do this, the brisket will be ready for smoking in 2 days.

Smoking: You will need a barbecue with a lid to trap the smoke and a thermometer to check the temperature.

FRIED CHICKEN SANDWICH

Makes **4** sandwiches

In an issue of Lucky Peach magazine, there was an article about foods that benefit from being chilled in the fridge overnight. The fried chicken rated the highest and got me thinking about other refrigerated leftovers that I love. They include cold sausage, pizza and meatballs. I will happily eat these in a sandwich, but mostly I just stand by the fridge with the door open and snack while keeping an eye out so I don't get busted by Beci.

With this sandwich, no more sneakiness is needed – it stands up in its own right. The smoked maple syrup is optional and will flip the taste completely. Of course, you can totally eat the fried chicken hot, but I prefer it cold in this sandwich. This is also the only time that I will say a light brioche roll is pretty ideal.

oil for deep-frying

150 g (5½ oz/1 cup) **self-raising flour**

2 teaspoons **hot paprika**

2 teaspoons **cayenne pepper**

2 teaspoons **mustard powder**

salt

750 g (1 lb 11 oz) **boneless chicken thighs**, skin left on, cut into even flat pieces

whole egg mayonnaise to serve

4 **brioche rolls** or soft white burger buns

smoked maple syrup to serve (optional) (see Recipe note)

CUCUMBER SALAD

2 **Lebanese (short) cucumbers**, seeded and shaved into ribbons

1 **small hot chilli**, thinly sliced

pinch of **poppy seeds**

1 **eschalot (French shallot)**, diced

1 tablespoon **white vinegar**

½ teaspoon **salt**

¼ teaspoon **caster (superfine) sugar**

1 tablespoon **olive oil**

lemon juice to taste

Heat the oil in a frying pan to 160°C (320°F), or until a cube of bread dropped into the oil turns golden brown in 25 seconds.

Combine the flour, paprika, cayenne pepper, mustard powder and 1 teaspoon of salt in a bowl. Coat the chicken with the flour mixture then give it a good shake to remove any excess flour.

Fry the chicken for 5–6 minutes on each side, or until the coating is crisp and golden brown and the chicken is cooked through. Drain on paper towel.

Lightly sprinkle salt over the chicken and try some to check the seasoning. Let the rest cool then put it in the fridge to chill. Pull the chicken out of the fridge 10–20 minutes before you want to serve it.

Meanwhile, make the cucumber salad. Combine all of the ingredients in a bowl and mix well. Refrigerate for 1 hour.

To assemble, spread some mayo on each brioche roll. Top with some of the cucumber salad and cold fried chicken, and drizzle over some maple syrup, if using.

Recipe note: You can get smoked maple syrup from specialty food stores.

STEAK SANDWICH

Makes **4** baguettes

Since the mid '90s, one of my favourite Melbourne restaurants has been Cicciolina. It's an Aussie spin on an Italian trattoria and the first few times I ate there I just couldn't put my finger on why I loved it so much. Sure, the food was amazing, but the small dining room was always packed and the wait for a table was always lengthy – and as a 19-year-old kid, I didn't care for waiting, nor did I care for white tablecloths. My good friend and long-time mentor, Phil Ransom, who looked out for me from when I left school at 16 until I got married at 27, would shout me a meal every week at Cicc'.

The restaurant was so busy they ended up turning their storeroom into a bar. This was a stroke of genius and before too long I was just meeting friends there to have a drink. One such friend was Beci who shared the same love for Cicciolina as Phil and me. Beci and I formed the basis of our relationship together over the tuna carpaccio and the roasted baby chicken while cramped into the corner of the bustling dining room. I cared not for restaurant reviews, hype or elitism – I cared for love and good vibes and this was exactly what was going down every time we pushed that side door open and stood awkwardly while they worked out if they had room for us.

Phil and I had a little queue-jumping scam. We would call Tascha, our friend on the inside, in the afternoon so she could get our names put in the queue. Whenever I would walk in with Phil, he would just hold up two fingers to Barb who runs the show and before too long there would be two steak sandwiches and a side of mash in front of us. I loved this sandwich so much I wanted to flip my own version as an ode to Cicciolina. Big thank yous to the team at Cicc' – Barb, Virginia, Simon and Tascha – for all the good times your restaurant showed me and my friends and family. I hope I get the chance to make this sandwich for you one day.

10 g (⅓ oz) dried sliced **porcini mushrooms**

20 g (¾ oz) **butter**

2 **eschalots (French shallots),** finely diced

2 **garlic cloves,** thinly sliced

4 **Swiss brown mushrooms,** finely chopped

1 teaspoon **thyme leaves**

salt

freshly ground **black pepper**

2 teaspoons **olive oil,** plus extra for drizzling

2 × 350 g (12½ oz) thick-cut **Scotch fillet (ribeye) steaks**

2 tablespoons **duck or chicken liver pâté,** or a combination of both

lemon juice to serve

4 × 15 cm (6 in) **baguettes,** halved lengthways

finely grated or prepared **horseradish** to serve

coriander (cilantro) leaves to serve

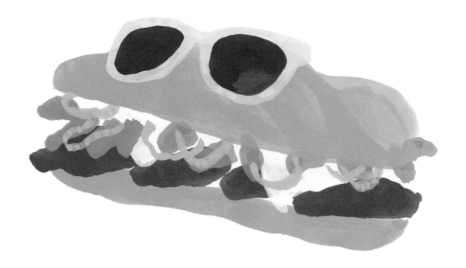

Soak the dried porcini mushrooms in 250 ml (8½ fl oz/1 cup) hot water for 30 minutes. Drain and reserve 125 ml (4 fl oz/ ½ cup) of the soaking liquid. Be careful not to include any of the sediment. Finely chop the porcini mushrooms.

Melt the butter in a frying pan over a medium heat. Fry the eschalot and garlic for about 1 minute, or until soft. Add the Swiss brown mushrooms and cook for 3–4 minutes, then add the porcini mushrooms, reserved soaking liquid and thyme. Season with salt and freshly ground black pepper and cook for 5–7 minutes, or until all of the liquid has evaporated and the mixture has become dry. Remove and let cool.

Bring a frying pan or chargrill pan to a medium–high heat. Rub 1 teaspoon of olive oil onto each steak, season with salt and freshly ground black pepper and cook for 4–5 minutes on each side for medium–rare, or until cooked to your liking. Transfer to a chopping board and let rest for 5 minutes.

Meanwhile, combine the mushroom mixture with the duck or chicken liver pâté in a bowl and smoosh it into a paste using a rubber spatula.

Slice the rested steaks and drizzle with some olive oil and a little lemon juice. To serve, spread some of the mushroom mixture onto one side of each baguette. Add slices of steak, a touch of horseradish, some coriander and top with the remaining baguette halves.

JERKY DOG

Makes *10–12* hotdogs

Homesick in London, or anywhere for that matter, is a feeling I'm sure many people have experienced. I was staying with my friend Gavin and I asked him what he did when he was needing some soul nourishment. He said he would always go by his mum's place for peas and rice. The next day he took me to a spot that wasn't as good as his mum's – of course – but that he rated as a proper jerk chicken, peas and rice place. It was exactly what I was looking for. The perfect comfort food. I returned every day for the remainder of the trip.

I created this jerky dog with that jerk chicken in mind. The flavours of the chicken are super bold and go great with the mango lime relish. You could also just grill the sausage and serve it with some fried plantains on the side.

10–12 **hotdog rolls**

JERKY DOG

½ teaspoon **ground cinnamon**

1 teaspoon freshly grated **nutmeg**

1 teaspoon **allspice**

1 **eschalot (French shallot)**

1 tablespoon **apple cider vinegar**

1 **Scotch bonnet or habañero chilli** (see Recipe notes)

10 g (¼ oz) **salt**

1 teaspoon freshly ground **black pepper**

1 kg (2 lb 3 oz) twice-minced (ground) **skinless, boneless chicken thighs** (see Recipe notes)

1 piece **caul fat** (see Recipe notes) or natural lamb casings, rinsed in cold water then soaked in lukewarm water for 1 hour

MANGO LIME RELISH

2 ripe **mangoes**, cut into chunks

juice of 5 **limes**

115 g (4 oz/⅓ cup) **honey**

60 ml (2 fl oz/¼ cup) **apple cider vinegar**

2 teaspoons finely grated fresh **ginger**

2 **eschalots (French shallots)**, thinly sliced

2 **garlic cloves**, thinly sliced

To make the mango lime relish, combine all of the ingredients in a saucepan and bring to the boil over a low heat. Cook, stirring occasionally, for 20–25 minutes, or until the sauce thickens. Transfer to a bowl and let cool to room temperature. Cover and refrigerate for at least 1 hour.

To make the jerky dog, combine the cinnamon, nutmeg, allspice, eschalot, apple cider vinegar, Scotch bonnet or habañero chilli, salt and pepper in a food processor and process until smooth. Transfer to a mixing bowl and add the minced chicken. Wearing gloves (as the chilli can get hectic), work the mixture with your hands until well combined. Divide the mixture into 10–12 equal-sized portions. If using casings, fill the casings using a sausage stuffer if you have one.

Alternatively, you can use a piping bag and a large plastic piping nozzle. Hold open the casings and run cold water through them. Gently slide one end of the casing over the end of the piping nozzle. Hold the loose casing with one hand and continue sliding the casing over the nozzle with the other hand, until there is about 5 cm (2 in) of casing left at the end. Fill the piping bag with about one-quarter of the mince mixture and twist the top of the bag. Use one hand to hold the casing on the nozzle and, with the other hand, gently pipe 5 cm (2¼ in) of the sausage mixture into the casing. Carefully squeeze out any air and tie a knot at the end of the casing, just beneath the filling. Continue piping until all of the mixture is used up. Refill the bag and pipe until the casing is full, being careful not to overfill the casing. Gently slide the casing off the nozzle and even out the filling using your fingers. Carefully squeeze out any air and tie a knot at the end of the sausage. Repeat the process with any remaining casings and mince mixture. Lay the filled casings on a work surface, then twist into links at 10 cm (4 in) intervals to make smaller sausages.

If using caul fat, spread out the caul fat on a work surface and cut it into 15–20 cm × 10 cm (6–8 in × 4 in) pieces. To make the sausages, divide the mixture between the caul fat pieces. Carefully roll into a sausage and tuck in the ends. Continue until all of the meat mixture is used up.

Cook the sausages in a frying pan over a low heat for 12–15 minutes, or until cooked through.

Serve the jerky dogs in the hotdog rolls and spoon over some of the mango lime relish.

Recipe notes: Scotch bonnet or habañero chillies: If you can't find fresh chillies, use dried chillies soaked in hot water for 20 minutes. You can get dried Scotch bonnets or habañeros from South American food stores.

Minced (ground) chicken: Ask your butcher to mince the chicken thighs twice, so they're really finely ground.

Caul fat: Ask your butcher for caul fat. It's the membrane of fat that surrounds the stomach of a pig, cow or sheep.

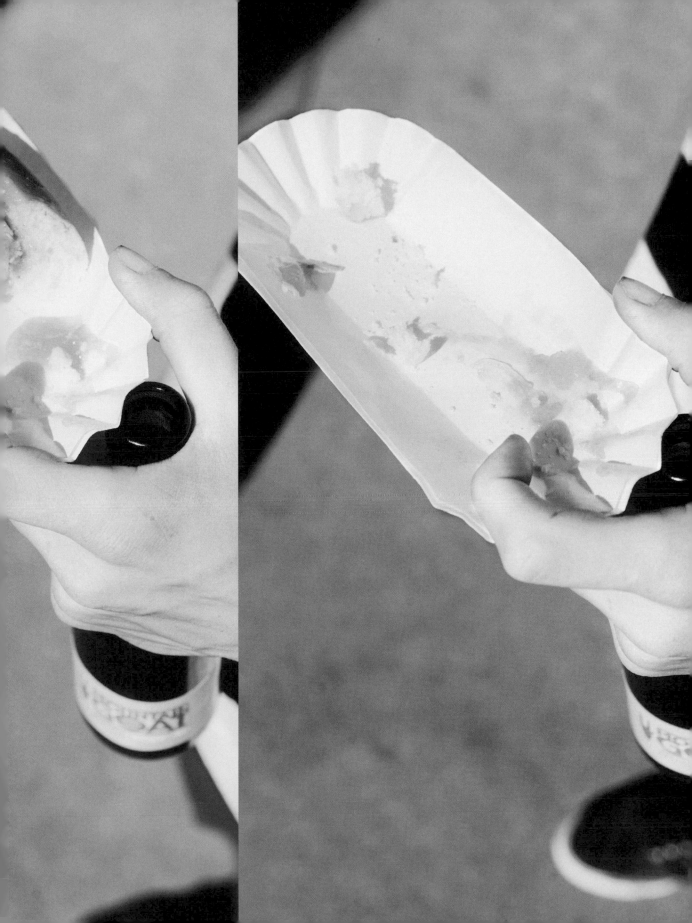

GRILLED FISH FILLET BURGER

Makes **4** burgers

160 g (5½ oz/⅔ cup) **whole egg mayonnaise**

1 tablespoon finely chopped **parsley**

1 tablespoon finely chopped **tarragon**

1 tablespoon freshly snipped **chives**

1 **gherkin (dill pickle),** finely chopped

2 **eschalots (French shallots),** diced

splash of **white wine vinegar**

1 tablespoon **oil**

700 g (1 lb 9 oz) **rockling** or any firm **white fish fillets,** about 1.5 cm (½ in) thick and cut into four 12.5 cm (5 in) squares

4 slices **processed cheese**

4 **burger buns**

In a small bowl, combine the mayonnaise, parsley, tarragon, chives, gherkin and eschalot. Give it a small hit of white wine vinegar and stir to make a tartare sauce.

Bring a small saucepan of water to the boil and arrange a wire rack over the top. Alternatively, use a steamer insert.

Heat the oil in a chargrill pan, frying pan or on a barbecue hotplate. Grill the fish over a medium heat for 3–4 minutes on each side, or until lightly browned and cooked through. In the last 5–10 seconds of cooking, put a slice of cheese on top of each fillet.

Cut the burger buns in half and lay the bread halves on the wire rack or steamer and steam for about 30 seconds.

To serve, put 1 fillet of fish into each burger bun and top with a big spoonful of the tartare sauce.

One of our staff members, Esther, took a holiday a couple of years back to go to a music festival overseas. I thought nothing of it, thinking she had gone to Glastonbury or Reading. About a month after she got back, I asked how Jay-Z had been at Glastonbury. She looked at me and said, 'Dude, I went to Worldwide Festival in Sete!'

'Um, OK. Sete ... um, where is that? Sounds French,' I mumbled. I thought I might as well keep rolling with the ignorance.

Esther started to hyperventilate slightly. 'OMG, so picture a music festival spread out over a little fishing town in the southeast of France, where fishermen catch and then cook you every meal from their little bistros, where there are shows in different venues all across town and the music just doesn't stop! Everyone is just chilled and on the same vibe.'

'Wow, sounds amazing!' I said, then started thinking of what I would make if I had a burger stand there. I would make this.

GRAPH

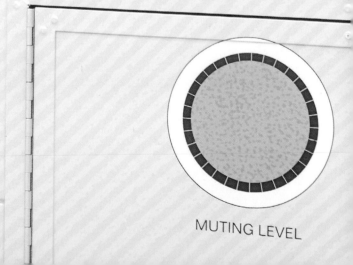

MUTING LEVEL

EGGPLANT SANDWICH WITH PICKLES AND HOT SAUCE

Makes *4* sandwiches

To make chipotle mayo, combine the mayonnaise with the chipotle in a bowl and mix well.

Lay the eggplant slices on paper towel and sprinkle with salt. Let sit for 15 minutes then wipe off any moisture. Dust the eggplant slices with plain flour, dip them in the egg and coat with the panko crumbs.

Heat the oil and butter in a frying pan over a low heat. Fry the eggplant slices for about 7–8 minutes on each side, or until golden brown, then drain.

To assemble, arrange the cabbage, avocado, coriander, eggplant, parmesan, red onion, gherkins and hot sauce, if using, on 4 slices of the sourdough. Top with the remaining slice of sourdough, with some chipotle mayo spread on the underside.

1 **eggplant (aubergine)**, sliced 1 cm (1/2 in) thick

salt

35 g (1¼ oz/¼ cup) **plain (all-purpose) flour**

1 large **egg**, beaten

60 g (2 oz/1 cup) **panko crumbs (Japanese breadcrumbs)**

60 ml (2 fl oz/¼ cup) **olive oil**

20 g (¾ oz) **butter**

thinly sliced **green cabbage** to serve

1 **avocado**, stoned and sliced

chopped **coriander (cilantro) leaves** to serve

grated **parmesan** to serve

thinly sliced **red onion** to serve

sliced **gherkins (dill pickles)** to serve

hot sauce to serve (optional)

8 slices **sourdough bread**

CHIPOTLE MAYO

125 g (4 oz/½ cup) **whole egg mayonnaise**

1 tablespoon finely chopped **chipotle en adobo** (see page 21)

Most Sundays I try to cook something. Whether it's a late lunch or early dinner, I generally have something on the go. Beci and I are super lucky to have lots of friends living in our neighbourhood and they know that our door is always open and there will be something to eat and drink. All of the dishes that I have put in the trucks have been developed in my kitchen at home, generally on the weekend when I have a bit more time to think about it and have people around to give me feedback. This sandwich came about one Sunday afternoon when I was just throwing some things together – sometimes I just like to make a few elements and put them on the table and let my friends decide what they want in their sandwich. It's when some awesome creations are made. This eggplant sandwich is one of them, put together by my friend Amanda.

My favourite companion for beef is onion. I can never get enough of onions when they are slowly sautéed; raw, on the other hand, I like just a hint of. This recipe lets you go as crazy as you like with the onion, as it's all cooked. I love the crispness, the steam and the sweetness. This burger is cooked in the style of an Oklahoma onion burger or even a New Jersey slider. Cooking the white onions on the patties imparts great flavour.

In a bowl, cover the white onion with water and set aside for 20 minutes. Drain.

Combine the flour, panko crumbs, a pinch of salt and 185 ml (6 fl oz) iced water in a bowl and whisk until smooth. If it's very thick add a little water, 1 teaspoon at a time. If it's very thin, add a little more flour.

Heat the oil in a deep-fryer or large heavy-based saucepan to 180°C (350°F), or until a cube of bread dropped into the oil turns golden brown in 15 seconds. Dredge the brown onion rings in the batter and fry for 1 minute, or until crunchy. Drain on paper towel.

Preheat the oven to 180°C (350°F).

Divide the minced meat into 4 equal-sized portions. With your hands, shape the portions into patties.

Heat the olive oil in a frying pan or chargrill pan until it's really hot. Salt the patties on one side and cook, salt side down. Top each patty with a small handful of the white onions and sprinkle with a little salt. Grill the patties for 2–3 minutes, or until there is a good crust. Flip and cook for 2–3 minutes, or until the onions are nicely charred. If adding cheese, melt some on the patties now.

Meanwhile, toast the buns then slice and spread with butter and mustard. Add some gherkin slices, a patty and a couple of brown onion rings. Pop on the bun tops and serve.

2 **white onions,** thinly sliced on a mandoline

75 g (2¾ oz/½ cup) **self-raising flour**

2 tablespoons **panko crumbs (Japanese breadcrumbs)**

salt

oil for deep-frying

1 **brown onion,** cut into 1 cm (½ in) thick rings

700 g (1 lb 9 oz) **minced (ground) chuck steak**

1 tablespoon **olive oil**

sliced **sharp cheddar** to serve (optional)

4 **burger buns**

butter to serve

favourite **mustard** to serve

sliced **gherkins (dill pickles)** to serve

ONION BURGER

Makes **4** burgers

SMOKED SHORT RIB SAUSAGE: 1 IN 1 OUT

Makes *10-12* sausage sandwiches

1 kg (2 lb 3 oz) **minced (ground) short rib** with 25 per cent fat ratio (see Recipe notes)

2 tablespoons **mustard powder**

1 tablespoon **sweet paprika**

½ teaspoon freshly ground **black pepper**

1 tablespoon **salt**

¼ teaspoon **garlic powder**

2 pieces **caul fat** (see Recipe notes)

90 g (3 oz/1 cup) **smoking woodchips,** soaked for 1 hour

2 tablespoons **oil**

3 **brown onions,** sliced

10-12 slices **white bread**

mustard to serve

tomato sauce (ketchup) to serve

Mix together the minced short rib, mustard powder, paprika, black pepper, salt and garlic powder in a bowl. Transfer half of the mixture to a food processor and start to process slowly. Add 60 ml (2 fl oz/¼ cup) iced water to the food processor to help the mixture combine. Transfer the mixture to a bowl and repeat the process with the remaining mince mixture. Divide the mixture into 10-12 equal-sized portions.

Spread out the caul fat on a clean work surface and cut it into 15-20 cm × 10 cm (6-8 in × 4 in) pieces. To make the sausages, divide the mixture between the caul fat pieces, carefully roll them into sausages and tuck in the ends. Continue until all of the meat mixture is used up.

To cook the sausages, prepare a stove-top smoker. Put the woodchips in a foil parcel, with an opening at the top to allow the smoke to escape. Put the parcel in a wok over a low heat. Arrange a 2-tier bamboo steamer basket over the top of the woodchips. Put the sausages into the top steamer basket and smoke over a low heat for around 15-20 minutes.

While the sausages are smoking, add the oil to a frying pan and sauté the onions over a medium heat until nicely browned, about 6-8 minutes. Transfer to a serving bowl and keep warm.

Heat the same frying pan until it's really hot. Transfer the sausages from the smoker into the frying pan. Cook for 2-3 minutes to crisp them up.

Serve the sausages in slices of white bread, topped with the onions, mustard and tomato sauce.

Recipe notes: Minced short rib: Ask your butcher to prepare the minced short rib with this ratio of fat.

Caul fat: Ask your butcher for caul fat. It's the membrane of fat that surrounds the stomach of a pig, cow or sheep.

I created this recipe in honour of Mike, my 'back of back of house guy' who stops the wheels falling off my whole operation. I met him a few years ago when I had the Beatbox truck at a music festival in country Victoria. It was midnight and we were busy. I could see that we were going to run out of sliced cheese for the burgers, so I grabbed a couple of wheels of gouda and set up the deli slicer and got to it. Another caterer at the event came past and saw me furiously slicing cheese. He said, 'Buddy there must be a better way.' I looked up and said, 'Yep, there is a better way. Be more organised.' He replied, 'OK, maybe I can help you out sometime.' That was Mike. Since then I have called on him nearly every other day. He understands my path and does his best to keep me on it.

In Australia, huge hardware stores have sausage sizzles out front, and it's pretty hard to resist the smell of sausages and onions, so I can guarantee that guys like Mike have one sausage on the way in and one on the way out.

I'm not trying to change the sausage at all. I even like the way the cook at the hardware store will burn a few edges while he or she waits for the next customers. But I do like the idea of making the sausage with better quality ingredients and giving it a little smoke. For me, it's all about the onions and quality beef.

LAMB RIB SANDWICH WITH RADICCHIO

Makes **4** sandwiches

I love ribs of all kinds. I think they are the perfect way to eat meat. My only concern is that they can be super fatty. I especially love lamb ribs. They are usually discarded at the butcher, but I really don't know why. My buddies in Japan don't like lamb too much, mainly because it smells way too rich. I tend to agree with them when it comes to mutton, but the lamb we get in Australia is generally always spring lamb and this is the same lamb that is exported. Spring lamb is way less full-on than older lamb or mutton. I like to cook the ribs almost to the point of falling off the bone, but I don't take it all the way as I still want the joy of chewing some meat off the bone. I pull apart some lamb for the sandwiches then also serve some ribs on the side.

5-6 **rosemary sprigs**
(about 15 cm/6 in long)

1 tablespoon **salt**

2 **lamb rib sections**
portioned into individual
ribs (around 18 lamb
ribs/1.2 kg/2 lb 10 oz)

250 g (9 oz/1 cup) **plain yoghurt**

handful of **mint leaves,**
chopped

butter lettuce to serve

thinly sliced **radicchio leaves** to serve

4 **sourdough** or **soft white rolls**

Preheat the oven to 140°C (275°F).

Make a rosemary brush by tying together the rosemary sprigs with kitchen string.

In a jar or bowl, dissolve the salt in 250 ml (8½ fl oz/ 1 cup) water.

Roast the lamb ribs in a roasting tin for 3½ hours. Using the rosemary brush, baste the ribs with the salt water every 30 minutes.

Combine the yoghurt with the mint in a bowl.

Mix together the lettuce and the radicchio – I like an 80/20 lettuce to radicchio ratio.

Increase the oven temperature to 220°C (430°F) for the last 10 minutes.

Cut the meat from the lamb ribs, remembering to leave a couple intact to chew on.

To assemble, put some salad leaves into each bread roll. Top with the shredded lamb, a dollop of minted yoghurt and serve with the lamb ribs on the side.

JALAPEÑO CHEESE MELT

Makes *1* cheese melt

100 g (3½ oz) **minced (ground) chuck steak**

sea salt

1 **eschalot (French shallot),** diced

butter to serve

2 slices **rye bread**

1 teaspoon **American mustard**

10 g (¼ oz) **pickled jalapeño** chopped

2-3 slices **provolone**

Heat a frying pan over a medium–high heat. Form the mince into a patty at least 10–15 per cent bigger than the bread slices. Lightly season the patty with sea salt and place in the pan. Top the patty with the eschalot and season with another pinch of sea salt. Cook for 2–3 minutes, or until a nice crust develops, then flip. The onions will start to char. Cook for another 1–2 minutes then remove the patty from the pan, making sure you scrape out all of the eschalot along with the patty. Let the patty rest for 1 minute.

Meanwhile, wipe the frying pan and reduce the heat to low.

Butter the bread slices, edge to edge, and add one piece of bread to the pan, butter side down. Spread the other side of the bread with mustard then top with the patty, eschalot, jalapeño, provolone and the remaining piece of bread, butter side up. I like to put a spatula on top of the sandwich and use an unopened tin of tomatoes as a weight to press down on the sandwich. I remove the weight once the cheese starts to melt. Cook the sandwich for 2–3 minutes per side, or until golden brown.

Grilled cheese is my go-to meal, especially if I'm in a breakfast-for-dinner type mood. This melt must be cooked in a pan or on a flat-top grill, with just a little bit of pressure to flatten the whole sandwich out and really melt the cheese.

MAINS

I have never been able to forward-plan a week of meals. In my endeavour to become more organised I have tried but it just never works out. The kids get fickle, someone wants to go vegetarian or I really just want to make pizza dough. These urges are what I base my day-to-day mains around. The only consistency in our kitchen is that we always sit down together at dinner time, my favourite time of the day.

COFFEE SAUSAGE AND EGG RAPH MUFFINS

Makes *12* muffins

When I first started the trucks, it was illegal for food trucks to trade in the City of Melbourne. In the early days, when I was full of gusto, I spent a lot of time at the council talking to them about my ideas and trying to convince them to change the law. Once every couple of months I would receive an email from someone on the council telling me they were really keen and the wheels were in motion to allow trucks and street vendors some access throughout the city. Unfortunately this started in '09 and we are still no closer to being granted access.

It was at these council meetings that I met Daniel the sausologist. His dream was also to build and trade from a truck, but the bureaucracy was really starting to kill his vibe. We would feel so deflated after the meetings and knew that it was going to be a while before anything changed. To give us something else to focus on, I suggested that we collaborate on a sausage. Even though we never got to serve this from his truck, I still hope it will wake some councillors up a bit.

12 **eggs**

butter, for spreading

MUFFINS

2½ teaspoons **dried yeast**

125 ml (4 fl oz/½ cup) **milk**

1 tablespoon **caster (superfine) sugar**

10 g (¼ oz) **vegetable shortening** or Copha

¼ teaspoon **salt**

375 g (13 oz/2½ cups) **plain (all-purpose) flour**

semolina for dusting

COFFEE SAUSAGES

150 g (5½ oz) **eschalots (French shallots),** sliced

2 tablespoons **olive oil**

50 g (1¾ oz) **unsalted butter**

500 g (1 lb 2 oz) **minced (ground) short rib** or **chuck steak** with 25 per cent fat ratio (see Recipe note)

125 ml (4 fl oz/½ cup) **pour-over (drip filter) coffee,** or 1 shot espresso topped with hot water

2 teaspoons **salt**

2½ teaspoons **finely ground coffee** (decaf is fine)

To make the muffins, combine the yeast and 125 ml (4 fl oz/ ½ cup) warm water in an electric mixer or food processor. Let stand for 10 minutes, or until the mixture starts to foam.

Meanwhile, gently heat the milk in a small saucepan over a low heat. Be careful to not let the milk boil. Add the sugar and stir to dissolve. Remove from the heat and let cool slightly. Add the milk mixture, shortening and salt to the yeast. Then add the flour and mix on low speed with a dough hook. Let the mixture combine and form a ball, then transfer to a lightly greased bowl. Cover with a tea towel (dish towel) and set aside in a warm place for about 30–40 minutes, or until the dough has doubled in size.

Knock back the dough and gently knead for 1–2 minutes. On a lightly floured work surface, roll out the dough until it is about 1 cm (½ in) thick. Use an egg ring to cut out 12 dough rounds. Cover and let rise for another 30 minutes.

Cook the eschalot in the olive oil and butter in a small saucepan over a low heat, until translucent and soft. Remove from the pan and let cool to room temperature before mixing with all the other sausage ingredients until combined.

Divide the sausage mixture into 12 equal-sized portions. Heat a non-stick frying pan, lightly oiled with cooking spray, over a low–medium heat. Sprinkle each round of dough with semolina and fry for 5 minutes on one side, or until lightly browned. Flip and cook the muffins for a further 3 minutes on the other side, or until cooked through. Remove from the pan and let cool.

Meanwhile, cook the sausage patties. Generally, I am pretty happy with the way things fall – sloppy is part of the charm for me – but I like to use an egg ring to shape the patties as I think it looks really neat.

Heat a non-stick frying pan over a low–medium heat. Place a couple of egg rings in the pan and oil them with a little cooking spray. Fill one ring with the sausage mixture and squish it down to make a patty. Cook for 3–4 minutes on each side, or until cooked through. Crack an egg into the other ring and cook for 2 minutes on each side. Repeat with the remaining sausage mixture and eggs. To finish, toast and butter the muffins. Place a sausage patty on each muffin, top with an egg and serve.

Recipe note: Ask your butcher to mince the short rib or chuck steak with 25 per cent fat.

If you have gone to the effort of curing, smoking and steaming a full brisket then you definitely need to eat these for breakfast the day after. As the briskets are around 2–3 kg (4 lb 6 oz–6 lb 10 oz) there are usually some leftovers to make these hash browns. I enjoy them so much that I'll make them for dinner, usually if I'm getting home late on a Sunday night and I am in a breakfast-for-dinner type mood. Even if you haven't done the full pastrami, you could use some store-bought pastrami … or, you could get your friend to make some and steal a little from them.

PASTRAMI HASH BROWNS

Makes **4**

2 **desiree**, or other **all-purpose potatoes**, halved

250 g (9 oz) **Pastrami** (see pages 114–115), chopped

2 tablespoons **plain (all-purpose) flour**

2 tablespoons **olive oil**

4 **eggs**

American or your **favourite mustard** to serve

hot sauce to serve (optional)

Bring a small saucepan of water to the boil. Add the potatoes and cook for 3 minutes. Drain and let cool for 5 minutes. Using a fine grater, grate the potatoes into a bowl. Add the pastrami and flour and mix to combine. Shape the mixture into 4 equal-sized patties.

Heat the olive oil in a non-stick frying pan over a low heat. Gently place the hash browns in the pan and fry for about 3–4 minutes, or until a crust has formed on the bottom. Flip and cook for another 3–4 minutes on the other side. Remove and drain on paper towel.

In the same frying pan, fry the eggs until cooked to your liking.

To serve, top each hash brown with some mustard, a little hot sauce, if using, and an egg.

POTATOES AND BEANS WITH CRACKED TORTILLAS

Serves *3-4*

200 g (7 oz) **dried black beans**, soaked overnight and drained, or 400 g (14 oz) **tinned black beans**

2 **guajillo chillies**, soaked in 500 ml (17 fl oz/ 2 cups) boiling water for 30 minutes

2 tablespoons **red wine vinegar**

145 ml (5 fl oz) **olive oil**

1 **red onion**, half diced, half cut into 5 mm (¼ in) thick slices

3 **garlic cloves**, thinly sliced

200 g (7 oz) **tinned tomatoes**

2 teaspoons **salt**

2 **potatoes**, cut into 5 mm (¼ in) thick slices

grated **Grana Padano** or parmesan to serve

2 **Corn tortillas** (pages 26-7), cut into matchsticks and fried until crispy (for method see page 153)

If using dried beans, add them to a saucepan with 1.5 litres (51 fl oz/6 cups) water and bring to the boil. Simmer, covered, over a medium heat for 30 minutes. Be careful not to overcook the beans – they shouldn't be fully cooked yet. Drain and refresh under cold water.

In a food processor or blender, combine the chillies, red wine vinegar and 250 ml (8½ fl oz/1 cup) of the chilli soaking liquid and process until smooth.

Heat 1 tablespoon of the olive oil in a saucepan over a low heat and fry the diced red onion and the garlic for 3–4 minutes, or until soft. Add the tinned tomatoes, guajillo chilli mixture, beans and salt. Bring to the boil then reduce the heat and simmer, covered, for 30 minutes, stirring occasionally. Remove the lid and simmer for 30 minutes if using dried beans, or 15–20 minutes if using tinned beans, or until the sauce has reduced and the beans are really tender.

While the beans are cooking, prepare the potatoes. In a frying pan over a low heat, gently fry the potatoes and the sliced red onion in 125 ml (4 fl oz/ ½ cup) olive oil. Cook, flipping every 5–10 minutes, for 20–25 minutes or until the potatoes are soft.

To serve, sprinkle a little cheese over the beans and top with the crispy tortilla strips. Serve with the potatoes.

VERDE MEATBALLS

500 g (1 lb 2 oz) **minced (ground) chicken or pork** with 20 per cent fat ratio (see Recipe notes)

3 tablespoons **spinach powder** (see Recipe notes)

2 teaspoons **salt**

1 bunch **coriander (cilantro)**, finely chopped

2 teaspoons **chilli flakes**

1 teaspoon **garlic powder**

1 tablespoon sliced **pickled jalapeño**

1 tablespoon **olive oil**

WHITE BEANS

3 teaspoons **olive oil**

7 **garlic cloves**, sliced

2 **rosemary stalks**, about 15 cm (6 in) long

800 g (1 lb 12 oz) tinned **cannellini (lima) beans**, drained

500 ml (17 fl oz/2 cups) **chicken stock**

VERDE MEATBALLS AND WHITE BEANS

Serves *4–6*

Most of the dishes I put together come from an idea to use an ingredient in a certain way or with a variety of other ingredients. This dish was inspired by colour. I wanted a contrast for the white beans and I thought verde (green) meatballs would be perfect.

To make the white beans, gently heat the oil, garlic and rosemary in a small saucepan or paella pan over a low heat for 2 minutes, or until the garlic is translucent. Stir in the beans then add the stock. Cook for 20–30 minutes, or until the mixture is thick and saucy, but the beans are still whole.

To make the verde meatballs, combine all of the ingredients except the olive oil in a food processor. With the motor running, slowly add 60 ml (2 fl oz/¼ cup) water and process until the mixture is the consistency of a paste. Shape the mixture into balls.

Heat the olive oil in a frying pan over a low heat. Cook the meatballs for 10–12 minutes, or until cooked through.

Serve the meatballs with the white beans.

Recipe notes: Minced (ground) chicken or pork: Ask your butcher to prepare pork or chicken mince with 20 per cent fat.

Spinach powder: You can get spinach powder from specialty food stores.

80 ml (2½ fl oz/⅓ cup)
cottonseed or canola oil

4 **Corn tortillas** (pages
26-7), cut into strips

½ **brown onion,** chopped

5 **garlic cloves,** crushed

1 quantity **Fire-roasted
salsa roja** (see page 76)

½ teaspoon **salt**

½ fresh or dried **habañero
chilli** (optional) (see
Recipe note)

½ teaspoon **ground cumin**

1 litre (34 fl oz/4 cups)
chicken stock

1 kg (2 lb 3 oz) **chicken
wings,** tips removed

chopped **avocado** to serve

grilled pineapple to
serve (for pineapple
grilling method see
page 64)

steamed **corn kernels**
to serve

roast potato cubes
to serve

chopped **coriander
(cilantro) leaves**
to serve

grated **Parmigiano
Reggiano** to serve

TORTILLA SOUP

Serves **4** as a main meal

Preheat the oven to 220°C (430°F).

Heat the oil in a large saucepan over a high heat. Fry the tortilla strips for 1 minute, or until crispy. Remove the strips and set aside.

Lower the heat to medium and let the oil cool slightly. Sauté the onion with the garlic for 2–3 minutes, or until translucent. Add the salsa roja, the salt and the habañero chilli, if using, and cook for 5 minutes. Add the cumin and the chicken stock and bring to a simmer. Reduce the heat to low and cook for 40 minutes, or until the tomatoes become really pulpy.

Meanwhile, roast the chicken wings in a roasting tin for 25 minutes, or until the wings are a dark golden brown and the chicken is cooked through. Strip the chicken meat from the bones, shred it into smaller pieces and keep warm until ready to serve.

To serve, strain the soup and divide into serving bowls. Add some of the chicken, avocado, pineapple, corn and potatoes as desired, scatter over the coriander and Parmigiano Reggiano and top with the crispy tortilla strips.

Recipe note: You can get dried habañero chillies from South American food stores.

FRIED CHICKEN WITH MUSTARD SAUCE AND BEANS

Serves *3–4*

My first food obsession was with fried chicken. As a kid my father made us ayam goreng – chicken deep-fried in coconut oil – which was so good I could never get enough. He used a combination of cumin and fresh turmeric to pop it.

I love that so many countries have their own version. As a teenager, my dream was to open up a restaurant called 'ILFC', short for 'International Language of Fried Chicken'. My idea was that every night I would do chicken from a different country. There'd be Southern Fried Tuesdays, Karaage Wednesdays, Gai Tod Thursdays, Ayam Goreng Fridays, Chicken Schnitzel Saturdays … you get the idea. The idea never came to fruition, but my love for fried chicken never died. So I got working on my own version. This dish takes cues from southern fried chicken with a nod to Japan's karaage. I like to serve it with dinner rolls, and some raw or blanched green beans.

1.2 kg (2 lb 10 oz) **chicken leg quarters,** bone in (see Recipe note)

150 g (5½ oz/1 cup) **plain (all-purpose) flour**

150 g (5½ oz/1 cup) **potato flour**

2 teaspoons **salt**

2 tablespoons **garlic powder**

2 teaspoons **paprika**

2 teaspoons **cayenne pepper**

vegetable shortening or **Copha** – enough for shallow-frying

8 **dinner rolls**

200 g (7 oz) **green beans,** blanched

BRINE

1 tablespoon **black peppercorns**

2 tablespoons **salt**

45 g (1½ oz/¼ cup lightly packed) **brown sugar**

½ bunch **coriander (cilantro) leaves** and **stems**

½ **lemon**

3 **garlic cloves**

1 **brown onion,** halved

3 **thyme sprigs**

MUSTARD SAUCE

185 g (6½ oz/¾ cup) **American mustard**

175 g (6 oz/½ cup) **honey**

60 ml (2 fl oz/¼ cup)
apple cider vinegar

1 tablespoon **brown sugar**

2 tablespoons
worcestershire sauce

To make the brine, combine all of the ingredients and 2 litres (68 fl oz/8 cups) water in a saucepan and bring to the boil over a medium heat. Lower the heat and simmer, covered, for 30 minutes. Remove from the heat and let the brine cool completely then refrigerate for 1 hour.

Cut the chicken pieces in half, separating the drumstick from the thigh.

Put the chicken pieces in the brine and refrigerate overnight. Drain the chicken pieces and rinse under cold water.

To make the chicken coating, combine the plain flour, potato flour, salt, garlic powder, paprika and cayenne pepper in a large plastic bag or a sealable plastic container. Add the chicken to the bag or container with the mixture. Shake until the chicken is well coated.

Heat the vegetable shortening in a frying pan over a low heat. Cook the chicken pieces for 8–10 minutes on each side, or until the coating is crispy and the chicken is cooked through. Be careful not to cook it too fast. It takes time and you have to stick with it.

Meanwhile, make the mustard sauce by whisking together the ingredients in a bowl until combined.

Serve the chicken with the mustard sauce, dinner rolls and green beans.

Recipe note: In Australia this cut of chicken is known as the maryland.

Fried Chicken with Mustard Sauce and Beans
Skirt Steak with Charred Spring Onions and Corn

1 tablespoon **ground cumin**

1 teaspoon **salt**

1 teaspoon freshly ground **black pepper**

1 tablespoon **olive oil**

500 g (1 lb 2 oz) **skirt (flank) steak**

2 **corn cobs,** cut in half

1 bunch **spring onions (scallions)**

60 g (2 oz/¼ cup) **whole egg mayonnaise**

grated **Grana Padano** to serve

beetroot (beet) powder to serve (see Recipe note)

SKIRT STEAK WITH CHARRED SPRING ONIONS AND CORN

Serves *2-3*

The only steak we ate growing up was skirt (flank) steak, which my parents would fry with soy beans and vegetables. They loved the flavour and the texture of the skirt and, as it was a secondary cut, and only really known to Asian restaurants, it was always pretty cheap. The muscle fibres are really pronounced, so you need to cut against the grain when slicing.

Skirt steak is really flavourful and takes all kinds of marinades well. I like to cook it two ways depending on how much time I have – either grill it quickly and serve it rare, or cook it low and slow in the oven at around 140°C for 3½ hours.

Combine the cumin, salt, pepper and olive oil in a small bowl. Rub the mixture all over the beef then cover it in plastic wrap and refrigerate for about 2 hours. Remove the steak from the fridge 30 minutes before you want to cook it to bring it to room temperature.

Blanch the corn in a saucepan of boiling water for 8–10 minutes.

Skirt steak is one of those cuts that you can either cook really quickly to medium–rare or really slowly over a few hours. Anywhere past medium–rare and the meat gets too tight. Below are instructions for both.

QUICK-COOKING METHOD

Heat a barbecue, chargrill pan or frying pan until it's really hot. Grill the skirt steak for 4–5 minutes on each side. While the skirt steak is cooking, grill the spring onions alongside it. When the steak is nicely browned, remove it from the heat and let it rest for 4 minutes. Continue cooking the spring onions until nicely charred. Add the blanched corn to the barbecue or pan and grill, turning, for 3–4 minutes. Spread the corn with mayo and sprinkle with Grana Padano and beetroot powder.

Slice the steak across the grain and serve with the corn and spring onions.

SLOW-COOKING METHOD

Preheat the oven to 140°C (275°F).

Heat a frying pan until it's really hot. Sear the skirt steak for 1–2 minutes on each side then transfer, along with any pan juices, to a small roasting tin. Add 125 ml (4 fl oz/½ cup) water to the tin, cover loosely with foil and roast in the oven for 3 hours. Remove the foil and cook for a further 30 minutes uncovered.

To prepare the spring onions and corn, preheat a barbecue, chargrill pan or frying pan to high. Char the spring onions and corn as above and spoon any pan juices onto the spring onions. Spread the corn with mayo and sprinkle with Grana Padano and beetroot powder.

Slice the steak across the grain and serve with the corn and spring onions.

Recipe note: You can get beetroot (beet) powder from specialty food stores.

3-4 **short rib strips**
(about 750 g/1 lb 11 oz
when trimmed), cut
1.5 cm (½ in) thick
(see Recipe note)

sea salt

QUICK PICKLED ONIONS

440 g (15½ oz/2 cups)
white sugar

625 ml (21 fl oz/2½ cups)
white vinegar

1 tablespoon **salt**

3 **red onions,** halved

My son's favourite beef cut is the short rib. He likes it when I roast it but prefers it sliced super thinly and quickly barbecued. The rib has a good amount of meat and fat. Give it a good charring and be sure to rest the meat. Once grilled, the excess fat can easily be cut off and discarded.

RIBS 'N' PICKLE

Serves *2*

For the quick pickled onions, combine the sugar, vinegar and salt in a small saucepan over a medium heat. Bring to a simmer and cook, stirring to dissolve the sugar, for 5 minutes. Remove from the heat and let cool.

Put the onions in a sterilised sealable jar. It doesn't have to be a pickle jar, but it does need to be airtight. Pour in the liquid and refrigerate overnight. These pickles will be ready to roll the next day.

To prepare the short ribs, preheat a barbecue or frying pan to medium–high. If cooking over charcoal, allow the fire to die down a bit to avoid flare-ups. Rub the ribs with a good pinch of sea salt, and cook for 7–8 minutes on each side, or until the ribs are nicely browned with some charred areas. Remove from the heat and rest for 5 minutes.

To finish, thinly slice the pickled onions and scatter over the short ribs. Spoon over some of the pickle juice and serve.

Recipe note: Get your butcher to slice the ribs up on the band saw.

This is just a little twist on the classic. My kids love chilli con carne and so do I.

CHILLI CON CARNE

Serves **6-8**

400 g (14 oz) tinned **black beans**, drained, or 220 g (8 oz/1 cup) **dried black beans**, soaked overnight and drained

2 tablespoons **olive oil**

1 **brown onion**, diced

5 **garlic cloves**, crushed

200 g (7 oz) **minced (ground) chuck steak**

300 g (10½ oz) **chuck steak**, trimmed and cubed

5 cm (2 in) piece **short rib**

400 g (14 oz) tinned **cherry tomatoes**

250 ml (8½ fl oz/1 cup) **beef stock**

2 teaspoons **ground cumin**

1 tinned **chipotle en adobo** and 1 tablespoon adobo sauce (see page 21)

salt

chopped **coriander (cilantro) leaves** to serve

steamed **rice** to serve

thinly sliced **radish** to serve

If using dried black beans, bring them to the boil in a saucepan with 1.5 litres (51 fl oz/6 cups) water. Simmer over a medium heat for 30 minutes, then drain.

Heat the oil in a deep saucepan or casserole over a low heat. Cook the onion and garlic for 4–5 minutes, or until translucent and soft. Add the minced and cubed chuck steak and stir until brown. Add the short rib piece, tinned tomatoes, beans, stock, cumin, chipotle and adobo sauce and stir well. Cover with a lid and simmer gently, stirring occasionally, for 2 hours. Remove the lid and simmer for a further 20–30 minutes, or until the liquid has reduced. Add salt to taste and scatter over the coriander.

Serve over steamed rice with some radish on the side.

BARBECUED GOAT RIBS

Serves **4**

2 **goat rib** sections
(about 600 g/1 lb 5 oz
each)

salt

1 **ruby grapefruit**, pith
removed and cut into 1 cm
(½ in) thick slices

1 **white onion**, thinly
sliced

stack of warmed **corn** or
flour tortillas to serve
(see pages 26–7)

BARBECUE SAUCE

125 ml (4 fl oz/½ cup)
tomato sauce (ketchup)

2 tablespoons **apple cider
vinegar**

125 ml (4 fl oz/½ cup)
worcestershire sauce

95 g (3¼ oz/½ cup,
lightly packed)
brown sugar

60 g (2 oz/¼ cup)
dijon mustard

Preheat the oven to 140°C (275°F).

Rub the skin side of the ribs with salt then put them in a roasting tin along with 250 ml (8½ fl oz/1 cup) water. Roast in the oven for 6 hours, checking on the amount of water in the pan and topping up as required.

Meanwhile, prepare the barbecue sauce. Mix together all of the ingredients with 60 ml (2 fl oz/¼ cup) water in a bowl until well combined.

During the last hour of cooking, baste the ribs with the barbecue sauce every 20 minutes.

Remove the ribs from the tin and let rest for 10 minutes. Slice into individual ribs and serve with the grapefruit, white onion and a stack of tortillas.

After reading the first MoVida cookbook by Frank Camorra, I was really keen to try out his recipe for goat. It worked out well but, since then, I have cooked goat a number of times with very mixed results. I have tried everything from slow-braising the shoulders to quick-grilling the cutlets – sometimes awesome, sometimes not so good. It got me thinking that perhaps my technique was okay but maybe my supply was to blame. I started to ask more questions of my butchers and it seemed that the goat industry in Australia was quite small and not a lot was known about the suppliers, let alone the breed of goat I was buying.

As I have been striving for complete transparency with all the suppliers that we buy from, I had to stop taking a gamble on the quality of goat until I could find out more. A good year passed until I discovered a farm 45 minutes from my house, named Seven Hills Tallarook. I called them up and they invited me to come and have a look around their picturesque farm where they breed Boer goats. The meat was so beautiful it inspired me to create this dish.

GLAZEY TAILS

Serves *4*

I often see oxtails in the butchers, as they are available pretty much all year round. Then, that one time when I really want them, they are always out of stock. It's like everyone gets the same idea for oxtail at exactly the same time. I swear there is a trigger in the temperature. When I can get my hands on them, this is my favourite thing to make.

Bring a heavy-based saucepan to a medium heat. Add the oil, 4 onion quarters, the ½ garlic bulb and oxtails and cook, stirring, for about 2 minutes, or until the tails have browned slightly. Add the salt, season with pepper and add enough water to cover (about 2.5–3 litres/ 85–101 fl oz/10–12 cups). Bring to the boil then reduce the heat and simmer for 1½ hours, checking intermittently and removing any scum that might come to the surface.

Remove the tails and let cool. Set aside 4 bone pieces and shred the meat from all the remaining tails then refrigerate. Strain the cooking liquid, reserving 750 ml (25½ fl oz/3 cups) and discard the rest. Refrigerate to cool and skim off the fat once it comes to the surface.

Preheat the oven to 200°C (400°F). Roast the tomatoes, the remaining onion quarters and garlic cloves and the chillies for 25–30 minutes, or until soft. Peel the garlic and then purée all of the roasted vegetables in a food processor or blender and add the cumin.

Increase the oven temperature to 250°C (480°F).

In a saucepan over a medium heat, simmer the reserved cooking liquid and the roasted vegetable purée until reduced by half. Add the oxtail meat, bone pieces, butter, lime juice and salt to taste and cook for a further 15 minutes. Transfer to a small roasting tin and roast in the oven for 15 minutes to give it some nice colour.

Serve with steamed rice.

1 tablespoon **oil**

1½ **brown onions,** quartered

½ **garlic bulb,** cloves crushed, plus 2 **garlic cloves,** unpeeled

1 kg (2 lb 3 oz) **oxtails**

2 teaspoons **salt**

freshly ground **black pepper**

2 **roma (plum) tomatoes,** halved lengthways

3 **guajillo chillies,** soaked for 30 minutes

1 teaspoon **ground cumin**

50 g (1¾ oz) **butter**

juice of ½ **lime**

steamed **rice** to serve

COLD FISH 'N' CHIPS

Serves **4**

When I was a kid, my family lived above our restaurant in Caulfield, southeast of Melbourne's CBD. On Saturday mornings I would be on bottle duty, which meant emptying all the bottles from the night before into the big bin in the back alley. Dumping bottles is super noisy and it would always wake up the neighbours who lived on the other side of the alley. Instead of getting grumpy, they would call me in to turn all of their lights on. I would race in and out, never thinking much of it. My mum later told me they would ask me to do this for religious reasons – being Jewish Orthodox, they observed the Sabbath and refrained from turning on electricity during this time. I remember at the time thinking, 'How do they cook? What do they eat?'

Ten years later, I was really getting into bagels and blintzes and I would head to the bagel shops in seaside St Kilda in Melbourne. Apart from the bagels, I always bought the cold fried fish. I loved it with just a little salt. I realised recently that cold fried fish is traditionally eaten on Shabbat and Jewish holidays, and I wanted to build a meal around it. I call it 'fish 'n' chips' cos it rings well, but really the potatoes are just roasted potatoes. This dish is great in summer and can obviously be prepared beforehand.

3–4 **all-purpose potatoes** (royal blue or sebago work well), cut into 1.5 cm (½ in) thick chips (fries)

2 tablespoons **olive oil**, plus extra for drizzling

250 g (9 oz) **green cabbage**, thinly sliced

juice of ½ **lemon**

2 tablespoons **dill**, finely chopped

1 kg (2 lb 3 oz) firm, white-fleshed **fish fillets** (whiting and flathead tails work well)

HUMMUS

125 g (4½ oz) **dried chickpeas (garbanzo beans)**, soaked overnight then drained

½ teaspoon **bicarbonate of soda (baking soda)**

2 **garlic cloves**, crushed

125 g (4½ oz) **tahini**

½ teaspoon **salt**

2 tablespoons **lemon juice**

2 tablespoons **iced water**

SALSA VERDE

1 bunch **coriander (cilantro)**

1 bunch **mint**

1 bunch **flat-leaf (Italian) parsley**

3 tablespoons **capers**

250 ml (8½ fl oz/1 cup) **olive oil**

½ **white onion**, thinly sliced on a mandoline

salt to taste

For the hummus, cook the chickpeas and bicarbonate of soda for 3 minutes. Add 750 ml (25½ fl oz/3 cups) water and bring to the boil. Cook, skimming any foam and loose skins that come to the surface, for about 30 minutes, or until the chickpeas are super tender. Drain well and transfer to a food processor or blender. Process the chickpeas into a paste, then add the garlic, tahini, salt and lemon juice and blitz again until combined. With the motor running, slowly drizzle in the iced water. The hummus will become really creamy within 1–2 minutes. Transfer to a bowl. Cover and let sit for 30 minutes, then refrigerate.

Preheat the oven to 180°C (350°F). Roast the potatoes with the 2 tablespoons of olive oil in a roasting tin for about 1 hour, or until the potatoes are crisp and cooked through.

Meanwhile, make the salsa verde. Wash and dry the herbs, then start chopping them on a large board. Add in the capers and continue chopping. Drizzle in the olive oil, bit by bit, continuing to chop and working the mixture back into the middle of the board. Continue adding the oil and chopping the herb mixture until all of the oil is incorporated. Transfer to a bowl and mix through the sliced onion.

In a bowl, combine the cabbage, lemon juice and dill to make a slaw. Drizzle with olive oil and toss.

Heat a barbecue or chargrill pan to medium–high. Lightly oil the cooking surface and grill the fish for about 3–4 minutes each side, or until cooked through. Let the fish cool then refrigerate. Remove the fish from the fridge 30 minutes before you want to eat it.

Serve the cold fish with the 'chips', salsa verde, hummus and slaw.

SALADS

While writing this book a lot of people have asked me what it's all about. I end up saying it's like taking a plane from the Queen Vic fresh produce market in Melbourne and flying over the Baja peninsula with a stop in LA and then on to NYC.

The Melbourne influence can be most prominently found in the next few salad pages. The quality of the vegetables and variety at the market means that Melbourne is always pushing great combinations and presentations of salads. I have found that fresh herbs are kinda like good manners – use them all the time and people will be happy.

FARRO SALAD WITH PICKLED TOMATOES AND SMOKED ALMONDS

Serves **4** as a main meal, **6** as a side dish

Unless you are smoking something else, it's kinda overkill to fire up the pit barbecue just for 1 cup of almonds, so I usually just fire up the stove-top smoker. All you need is a wok, a bamboo steamer and some smoking woodchips.

200 g (7 oz/1 cup) **farro**

handful of **coriander
(cilantro) leaves,**
chopped

pinch of **salt**

extra-virgin olive oil,
for drizzling

SMOKED ALMONDS

155 g (5½ oz/1 cup)
raw almonds

1 teaspoon **raw caster
(superfine) sugar**

½ teaspoon **peanut oil**

90 g (3 oz/1 cup) **smoking
woodchips,** soaked for
1 hour

habañero sauce to taste

PICKLED TOMATOES

125 ml (4 fl oz/½ cup)
apple cider vinegar

60 ml (2 fl oz/¼ cup)
white vinegar

1 tablespoon **salt**

1 tablespoon **sugar**

1 **garlic clove**

1 teaspoon **black
peppercorns**

250 g (9 oz) **cherry
tomatoes,** halved

To make the pickled tomatoes, combine the apple cider vinegar, white vinegar, 190 ml (6½ fl oz/¾ cup) water, salt, sugar, garlic and peppercorns in a saucepan. Bring to the boil over a medium heat, then reduce the heat and simmer for 5 minutes. Remove from the heat and let cool.

Put the cherry tomatoes in an airtight container and cover with the pickle juice. Refrigerate for 24 hours, or more if you have the time. These will be good for 3–4 days.

For the smoked almonds, combine the almonds, sugar and oil in a mixing bowl and toss to coat the nuts. To make a stove-top smoker, put the woodchips in a foil parcel, with an opening at the top to allow the smoke to escape. Put the parcel in a wok over a low heat. Arrange a bamboo steamer basket over the top of the woodchips. Once the smoker starts smoking, spread out the almonds over the base of the bamboo steamer and cook with the lid on for 30 minutes. Check periodically to make sure the almonds aren't getting too dark. Remove from the basket and let cool for 30 minutes, or until the almonds go super crunchy. Add a splash of habañero sauce.

In a saucepan, bring the farro and 750 ml (25½ fl oz/3 cups) water to the boil. Cook, covered, for 20–30 minutes, or until the farro is cooked to your liking. I like it with a bit of bounce, so I usually only cook it for 20 minutes.

Drain and refresh the farro under cold water, then drain again.

To make the salad, roughly chop the smoked almonds then combine with the farro, half of the coriander and about 10–12 pickled tomato halves in a bowl and mix well. Add a good pinch of salt and drizzle over some olive oil. Top with the rest of the coriander and serve.

My favourite cookbook from the last few years would have to be Jerusalem by Yotam Ottolenghi and Sami Tamimi. I happily recommend it all the time. It's just one of those books that I feel has something for everyone. After cooking from it a few times a week for about a month, I ended up with quite a stash of spice mixes that were left over from some of the recipes. I started to work the excess spice mixes into some of my own dishes. This is my favourite.

ZUCCHINI AND CHICKPEA SALAD

Serves *2* as a main meal, *4* as a side dish

2-3 **zucchini (courgettes),** diced

1 tablespoon **olive oil,** plus more for drizzling

2 tablespoons **tahini**

2 tablespoons **sour cream**

lime juice to taste

¼ teaspoon **salt**

400 g (14 oz) **tinned chickpeas (garbanzo beans),** drained

handful of chopped **mint**

handful of chopped **coriander (cilantro) leaves**

thinly sliced **red onion** to serve

SPICE MIX

1 teaspoon freshly ground **black pepper**

1 teaspoon **allspice**

1 teaspoon **ground cumin**

½ teaspoon **ground coriander**

1 teaspoon **dried oregano**

To make the spice mix put all the ingredients in a small bowl and mix well.

In a separate bowl, combine the zucchini, the olive oil and the spice mix.

Cook the zucchini mixture in a frying pan over a medium heat for 6–7 minutes, or until tender. Transfer to a bowl and let cool.

Whisk together the tahini, sour cream, lime juice and salt in a bowl. If the tahini cream is too thick, add 1 teaspoon water to loosen.

Add the chickpeas and the tahini cream to the cooled zucchini mixture and mix well. Add another squeeze of lime and the mint and coriander leaves and toss. Top with slices of red onion and sprinkle over a pinch of salt. Drizzle with a little more olive oil and serve.

POTATO AND CORN SALSA

Serves *6–8*

4 **corn cobs**

150 ml (5 fl oz) **canola oil**

2 **potatoes,** unpeeled and diced

salt

1 teaspoon finely grated fresh **ginger**

1 tablespoon **olive oil**

1 tablespoon **lemon juice,** plus more to taste

1/4 cup chopped **coriander (cilantro) leaves**

1/2 **white onion,** diced

Bring a saucepan of water to the boil. Cook the corn for 10–12 minutes, then drain and let cool. Slice off the kernels.

Heat the canola oil in a frying pan or saucepan over a low–medium heat. Fry the potatoes, stirring occasionally, for 15 minutes or until crispy. Let cool and sprinkle over a little salt.

Whisk together the ginger, olive oil and lemon juice.

Mix together the corn, potatoes, coriander and onion and the ginger dressing in a bowl. Add more lemon juice if needed and serve.

Zucchini and Chickpea Salad
Potato and Corn Salsa

BURRATA AND BABY BEETROOT WITH ROASTED HAZELNUTS

Serves *2* as a main meal, *4* as a side dish

20-25 **baby beetroot (beets)**

35 g (1¼ oz/¼ cup) unsalted **roasted hazelnuts,** halved

2 teaspoons **olive oil**

2 teaspoons **apple cider vinegar**

1 **burrata**

Preheat the oven to 180°C (350°F). Put the beetroot in a small roasting tin and cover with foil. Depending on the size of the beetroot, roast for about 1 hour, or until cooked through.

Refresh the beetroot under cold water then remove the skins. In a bowl, combine the beetroot with the hazelnuts, oil and apple cider vinegar and mix well. Transfer to a plate and top with the burrata.

Burrata and beetroot (beets) is a great pairing. Burrata is a fragile mozzarella ball. The outer shell is mozzarella and it is filled with cream and more mozzarella. Some can be more fragile than others, so handle with care. When everyone sits down at the table, ask for a moment of silence while you all witness the breaking of the burrata. It's a beautiful thing.

CLAM SALAD WITH PINK GRAPEFRUIT AND CORIANDER

Serves *2*

I love any food that you have to eat with your hands. Use the clam shells to scoop up a little potato, chilli and grapefruit.

1 **potato,** diced into 1 cm (½ in) cubes

3 **garlic cloves,** thinly sliced

2 tablespoons **olive oil**

1 kg (2 lb 3 oz) **clams (vongole)**

1 **ruby grapefruit,** pith removed and cut into segments

handful of **coriander (cilantro) leaves,** chopped

freshly ground **black pepper**

thinly sliced **bird's eye chilli,** to serve (optional)

In a small saucepan of water over a medium heat, boil the potato for 7–8 minutes, or until tender. Drain the potato.

In a frying pan over a low–medium heat, gently soften the garlic in the olive oil. Add the potatoes and clams and toss them through the garlic. Cook for about 7–10 minutes, or until all the clams have opened. Discard any unopened clams.

Transfer the salad to a serving platter and spoon over 4–5 tablespoons of the cooking liquid from the pan. Top with the ruby grapefruit, coriander, a crack of black pepper and the sliced chilli, if using.

105 g (3½ oz / ¾ cup) **pepitas (pumpkin seeds)**

1 teaspoon **peanut oil**

½ teaspoon **cayenne pepper**

1 teaspoon **salt**

½ teaspoon **raw caster (superfine) sugar**

1 kg (2 lb 3 oz) **chicken wings**

1 tablespoon **ghee**

2 **garlic cloves**, thinly sliced

200 g (7 oz/1 cup) **basmati rice**, washed

250 ml (8½ fl oz/1 cup) **chicken stock**

250 ml (8½ fl oz/1 cup) **milk**

sea salt

1 bunch **coriander (cilantro) leaves**, chopped

lime juice to taste

favourite hot sauce to taste

Preheat the oven to 200°C (400°F).

Combine the pepitas, oil, cayenne pepper, salt and sugar in a bowl then spread out the mixture on a baking tray. Roast for 10–15 minutes, checking occasionally to make sure it doesn't burn. Remove from the oven and let cool.

Sprinkle the chicken wings with a good pinch of salt and roast in the oven in a roasting tin for 30 minutes, or until they are nicely browned and the chicken is cooked through. Let the wings cool then shred the meat with a fork. Discard the bones.

Melt the ghee in a frying pan over a low heat. Fry the garlic for 1–2 minutes, or until softened. Add the basmati rice and stir well to coat the rice in the ghee. Add the stock and the milk and cover, with the lid ajar, and bring to the boil. Once boiling, cook for 2–3 minutes, then cover completely with the lid and turn off the heat. Let sit for 15 minutes.

Fold half the pepita mixture and a good pinch of sea salt through the rice then top with the shredded chicken, the coriander and the remaining pepita mixture. Give it a good squeeze of lime and a hit of your favourite hot sauce and serve.

CHICKEN RICE WITH SPICED PEPITAS

Serves **4**

*This is a bit of a winter salad. When I make it in summer,
I just flip the mandarin for valencia orange or mango.*

GRILLED CAULIFLOWER WITH MANDARIN, HAZELNUTS AND AVOCADO

Serves **4** as a main meal,
6 as a side dish

4 **eschalots (French shallots),** sliced

80 ml (2½ fl oz/⅓ cup) **olive oil**

1 teaspoon **sugar**

1 tablespoon **white vinegar**

salt

1 small **cauliflower** (about 800 g/1 lb 12 oz), cut into florets

1 **avocado,** stone removed and flesh roughly chopped

70 g (2½ oz/½ cup) unsalted **roasted hazelnuts,** halved

2 **mandarins,** separated into segments then cut in half

handful of **coriander (cilantro) leaves,** chopped

Combine the eschalot, oil, sugar, vinegar and a pinch of salt in a small bowl and set aside for 1–2 hours.

Preheat a barbecue or chargrill pan to a medium heat. Cook the cauliflower for 15–20 minutes, or until tender, then set aside to cool.

In a bowl, combine the eschalot mixture, cauliflower, avocado, hazelnuts, mandarin segments and coriander. Toss well and serve.

Generally when I return home from working a big multi-day festival, I am pretty run down. For a few days, the only things I crave are vegetables, but I'm usually too exhausted to cook. I often give my friend Kirra a call and she comes through with some raw foods, like bunches of kale and all types of green drinks. I always feel better for it. If Kirra comes to our place, I usually make her this.

LENTIL SALAD WITH CARAMELISED ESCHALOTS

Serves **4**

185 g (6½ oz/1 cup) **green lentils**

4 **eschalots (French shallots),** sliced

80 ml (2½ fl oz/⅓ cup) **olive oil**

80 g (2¾ oz) **bocconcini,** torn

1 teaspoon **chilli flakes**

handful of **mint,** chopped

6–8 **cherry tomatoes,** halved (optional)

1½ teaspoons **sea salt**

freshly ground **black pepper**

In a saucepan, cover the lentils with water and bring to the boil over a medium heat. Cook for 18–20 minutes, or until just cooked through. Drain and set aside to cool.

In a frying pan over a low heat, gently cook the eschalot in the oil for about 15–20 minutes, or until they are a nice dark brown. Stir every few minutes to make sure they're not sticking or burning. Transfer the eschalot and the oil to a serving bowl. Add the lentils, bocconcini, chilli flakes, mint, cherry tomatoes, if using, salt and freshly ground black pepper to taste. Mix well and serve.

SWEETS

My favourite dining term of all time is the Japanese word betsubara, *which translates to, 'Even if I am full, I have an extra stomach just for dessert.'* Beci has pulled this word out many a time when everyone else at the table is a bit 'whatever' about ordering dessert. 'We can just get a couple to share. Betsubara!' She can be very convincing. She is right, though; desserts are always great when you share them.

Dessert doesn't have to be over the top in portion size. Most of the time I am happy with a spoonful of ice cream with a sprinkling of Milo. I love making donuts for parties – be sure to glaze them in front of everyone, as it's mesmerising.

Melaka is a small historic town about two hour's drive south of Kuala Lumpur in Malaysia. It's really pretty and happens to be the place where my father passed away. I returned to Melaka for my father's wake. He had been running, and living at, the local art gallery; an open-air type of gallery with a couple of big rooms for students to exhibit work. He and his students had their paintings and theories all over the place. The caretaker of the gallery gave me his last drawing (pictured below) of a split-open durian fruit. The walls of the gallery were a really distinct purple.

A few years ago, I was playing around with some chia seeds and I stirred some coconut milk through them. After you let them sit for a while, this great colour comes about. This is the colour of the gallery. Sympathetic to the local dessert of gula melaka, I thought it best I top this dish with syrupy palm sugar.

45 g (1½ oz/¼ cup) **white chia seeds**

45 g (1½ oz/¼ cup) **black chia seeds**

400 ml (13½ fl oz) **coconut milk**

200 g (7 oz) **palm sugar (jaggery)** (dark, crumbly palm sugar works best)

CHIA MELAKA

Serves **4–5**

Combine the white chia seeds, black chia seeds and coconut milk in a bowl. Cover and refrigerate for about 1 hour, or until the pudding sets. Stir the mixture every 15 minutes.

Meanwhile, in a saucepan over a low heat, melt the palm sugar in 80 ml (2½ fl oz/⅓ cup) water, stirring occasionally, until the mixture is syrupy.

Serve the pudding in glass bowls and spoon over the desired amount of palm sugar syrup.

MALTED CARDAMOM SHAKE

Serves *2*

Bruise the cardamom pods then combine them with the ground cardamom and milk in a heavy-based saucepan. Bring to the boil then simmer over a low heat for 3–4 minutes. Transfer the milk mixture to a bowl and let it cool slightly, then cover with plastic wrap and refrigerate for 1–2 hours.

Strain the cooled milk mixture and whiz in a food processor with the ice cream and malt extract until thick and well combined.

Serve over ice.

BANOFFEE GINGER CONE

Makes **6** cones

This is just a little twist on the classic pie. Ian Dowding and Nigel Mackenzie, who are credited with creating the banoffee pie in England in 1972, have gone on to say they disapprove of it being made with cookie-crumb bases and aerosol cream. They seem to be cool with using condensed milk from the can and instant coffee, though. All good with me. I've tried not to upset them too much with this rendition.

2 ripe **bananas**, sliced lengthways

CONES
(see Recipe notes)

2 **egg whites**

95 g (3¼ oz/½ cup, lightly packed) **brown sugar**

½ teaspoon **natural vanilla extract**

⅛ teaspoon **salt**

100 g (3½ oz/⅔ cup) **plain (all-purpose) flour**

40 g (1½ oz) **unsalted butter**, melted

¼ teaspoon **ground cinnamon**

¼ teaspoon **freshly grated nutmeg**

¼ teaspoon **ground ginger**

1 tablespoon **milk**

COFFEE CREAM

300 ml (10 fl oz) **thickened (whipping) cream**

½–1 teaspoon finely **ground coffee**

DULCE DE LECHE
(see Recipe notes)
1 litre (34 fl oz/4 cups) **goat's milk or full-cream (whole) milk**

110 g (4 oz/½ cup) **white sugar**

2.5 cm (1 in) piece **cinnamon stick**

¼ teaspoon **bicarbonate of soda (baking soda)**, dissolved in 1 tablespoon water

Put the banana slices in the freezer for 3 hours, or until they are frozen.

To make the cones, combine the egg whites, sugar and vanilla extract in a small mixing bowl. Stir in the salt and half of the flour, then mix in the melted butter. Using an electric beater, beat in the remainder of the flour and the cinnamon, nutmeg, ginger and milk. Heat a waffle iron and lightly oil with cooking spray. Place ⅙ of the batter in the iron and cook for 45 seconds on each side. Roll the waffle onto a cone roller and let cool. Repeat with the remaining batter.

To make the coffee cream, whip the cream until semi-stiff peaks form then fold in the coffee. Refrigerate until needed.

To make the dulce de leche, combine the milk, sugar and cinnamon stick in a saucepan. Stirring constantly, bring the mixture to a simmer over a low–medium heat. This should take about 2–3 minutes. Once simmering, remove the pan from the heat and stir in the bicarbonate of soda. It might bubble up a bit. Once the bubbles die down, return the pan to a low–medium heat and bring the mixture to an even simmer, making sure it's not simmering too gently. Cook, stirring frequently, for 1 hour, or until the mixture becomes a golden caramel colour and is the consistency of thick honey. As the colour starts to change, be sure to stir more frequently to prevent sticking. Stir until you reach your desired consistency and colour. Strain the mixture then let cool.

To serve, dunk the collar of the cone into the dulce de leche then spoon 1 teaspoon of dulce de leche into the cone. Top with two slices of banana and fill with the coffee cream.

Recipe notes: Cones: If you don't have a waffle iron, just buy 6 waffle cones from your local ice cream store.

Dulce de leche: If you are short on time, you can make a cheat's version of dulce de leche. Bring a saucepan of water to the boil. Once boiling, reduce to a simmer and add an unopened 400 g (14 oz) tin of sweetened condensed milk. Cook, covered, for 1–1½ hours. Make sure that there is always enough water to cover the tin. Drain and let the tin cool for 5–10 minutes before opening. If the dulce de leche becomes too thick, beat it using an electric mixer for 1–2 minutes, or until the lumps have dissolved and the dulce de leche is smooth.

Banoffee Ginger Cone

ICE CREAM CONES AT THE MOVIES

Makes *6* cones

I don't get to the cinema a whole lot these days, but I enjoy it when I do. Now, my brother Rudin REALLY loves the movies. All sorts. Everything he sees is the best film he has ever seen. He just loves films. Last time I rolled with him we caught a 9.15 pm session. As I scooped up the tickets, Rudin was at the snack shop filling up both arms with giant bags of popcorn. I was like, 'Dude, I had dinner.' As we walked towards the cinema, he looked back at me, carrying two barrels of awkward goodness in his arms, and said, 'Whatever Man, this is just a little something.'

As the movie started rolling, Rudin, the keeper of the snacks, threw me a choc top ice cream. I settled in and took a delicious bite. He gave me a nudge and whispered, 'This is what's up.' I turned to see that he had eaten off the choc outer layer and was dunking his whole ice cream in the popcorn box. I followed his lead. Salty, creamy, buttery, chocolatey ... yep, I was definitely in with this. Four dunks and I was done.

100 g (3½ oz/½ cup) **popcorn kernels**

2 tablespoons **vegetable oil**

sea salt

6 **ice cream cones**

1 litre (34 fl oz/4 cups) **vanilla ice cream**

SALTED CARAMEL

100 g (3½ oz) **caster (superfine) sugar**

50 g (1¾ oz) **butter**

1 teaspoon **salt**

To make the popcorn, add the popcorn kernels and vegetable oil to a saucepan over a low heat. Cover with a lid and once the kernels start to pop, give the saucepan a shake then leave the lid very slightly ajar. Listen carefully to the frequency of the pops – when there are a few seconds between pops, remove from the heat.

To make the salted caramel, combine all of the ingredients and 60 ml (2 fl oz/¼ cup) water in a small heavy-based saucepan and bring to the boil over a low heat. Cook, scraping down the side of the saucepan with a rubber spatula, for about 10–12 minutes, or until the sugar starts to change colour to golden brown. Remove from the heat and stir the caramel for about 45 seconds.

Spread out the cooked popcorn on a baking tray and drizzle over the caramel. Hit it with 2 good pinches of sea salt and let it cool.

To serve, top each cone with 1 scoop of vanilla ice cream. Divide the popcorn into serving bowls and serve with the ice cream cones so each person can dip as desired.

HORCHATA PIE WITH LIME CURD

Serves **6**

Horchata is a creamy, refreshing drink that I love served over ice. Most taquerias serve it alongside other house-made drinks, in big countertop barrels.

HORCHATA

500 ml (17 fl oz/2 cups)
rice milk

40 g (1½ oz/¼ cup)
raw almonds

1 **cinnamon stick**

100 g (3½ oz) **white sugar**

50 g (1¾ oz) **brown sugar**

20 g (¾ oz) **milk powder**

15 g (½ oz) **cornflour
(cornstarch)**

100 g (3½ oz) **unsalted
butter,** melted

8 **egg yolks**

300 ml (10 fl oz) **pouring
(single/light) cream**

BISCUIT (COOKIE) BASE

125 g (4½ oz) **ginger nut
biscuits (ginger snaps)**

75 g (2¾ oz) **Nice
biscuits (plain sugar
cookies)**

40 g (1½ oz) **rolled oats**

100 g (3½ oz) **unsalted
butter,** melted

LIME CURD

4 **eggs**

zest and juice of 2 **limes**

100 g (3½ oz) **butter,**
chopped into 1 cm (½ in)
cubes

330 g (11½ oz/1½ cups)
white sugar

To make the horchata, gently simmer the rice milk, almonds and cinnamon stick for 10 minutes in a saucepan over a low heat. Pour the mixture into a bowl and let it cool for 30 minutes. Cover and refrigerate for at least 2 hours, or preferably overnight.

Once chilled, whiz the horchata in a food processor for 1–2 minutes, then strain and discard the solids.

Preheat the oven to 160°C (320°F).

To make the biscuit base, blitz the biscuits and rolled oats in a food processor for 1–2 minutes, then add the melted butter and process until combined. Press the mixture into the base and side of a 23 cm (9 in) pie tin.

Using a stand mixer on a low setting, mix the white sugar, brown sugar, milk powder and cornflour until combined. Add the melted butter and continue to mix on low. Add the horchata rice milk mixture and mix. Add the egg yolks and mix until incorporated, then add the cream. Pour the mixture into the pie tin and bake for 30 minutes, or until the middle is just set. Cool, and freeze overnight.

To make the lime curd, whisk the eggs, lime zest, lime juice, butter and sugar in a heavy-based saucepan or over a double boiler. Cook the mixture slowly over a low heat, whisking continuously for around 15–20 minutes, or until the mixture is thick and smooth. Don't let it boil or it may separate. Let the mixture cool, then refrigerate for 1 hour.

When ready to serve, remove the pie from the freezer and let it stand at room temperature for 10 minutes. Slice and serve with the lime curd.

1 tablespoon **cornflour**
(cornstarch)

375 ml (12¹/₂ fl oz/1¹/₂ cups)
milk

250 ml (8¹/₂ fl oz/1 cup)
pouring (single/light)
cream

75 g (2³/₄ oz/¹/₃ cup)
sugar

¹/₄ teaspoon **salt**

375 ml (12¹/₂ fl oz/
1¹/₂ cups) **Coca-Cola**

2 tablespoons **glucose**
or **corn syrup**

¹/₂ **vanilla bean,** split
lengthways and seeds
scraped

60 g (2 oz/¹/₄ cup)
cream cheese

12 **ice block (popsicle)**
sticks

In a bowl, stir together the cornflour and
60 ml (2 fl oz/¼ cup) of the milk to make a slurry.
Set aside.

Whisk together the remaining milk, the cream,
sugar, salt, Coca-Cola and glucose in a small
saucepan. Scrape the seeds of the vanilla bean
into the mixture and whisk until combined. Bring
the mixture to the boil over a low heat then stir
in the cornflour slurry. Cook, stirring, for about
2–3 minutes, or until thickened.

In a bowl, combine the cream cheese with
60 ml (2 fl oz/¼ cup) of the hot liquid and whisk
until smooth. Stir in the remaining mixture. Cover
the mixture with plastic wrap and refrigerate for
1 hour.

Once completely chilled, pour the mixture into
an ice cream maker and churn according to the
manufacturer's instructions.

Divide the churned mixture between 12 ice block
(popsicle) moulds and insert a wooden ice block stick
into the base of each ice cream. Place in the freezer
to set.

VANILLA COKE
ICE CREAM STICK

Makes *12* ice creams

DONUTS

Makes *12–14* donuts

I didn't start drinking coffee until our first son, Tyke, was born. He would wake up super early and one morning I decided to dust off a little stove-top coffee pot that we had been given for a wedding present. Coffee had always seemed way too strong and bitter for my liking, and I didn't see the value in adding lots of sugar and milk to change it. I usually just drank tea, but I loved the smell of coffee when it was being made.

Using the stove-top pot, I still found the coffee way too strong, even with a bit of water added to weaken it. I started to order coffees from various places around town to see how my home brews were stacking up. I honestly couldn't tell. I found the coffee really harsh everywhere I went, unless it was white with a sugar. Lattes seemed to be the most popular and long blacks with extra water were getting no love.

I gave coffee a rest for a bit but the smell was so tempting that even bad coffee was hard to resist. Beci started doing some graphics for a coffee roaster called Seven Seeds. They introduced specialty coffee beans to Melbourne. I got to try a whole bunch of great coffees and realised that I love a pour-over (drip filter).

Now I drink coffee once a day and my favourite thing to have with coffee is a donut. I love coffee with donuts. Here's a recipe that I think works perfectly.

Mix 1 teaspoon of the yeast, 250 ml (8½ fl oz/1 cup) warm water, the egg and 225 g (8 oz/1½ cups) of the flour together with a whisk until smooth. Cover and let stand in a warm place for 1 hour or until small bubbles start appearing on the surface.

Combine this mixture with the remaining flour and yeast, the sugar, milk, salt and vanilla in a stand mixer with a dough hook and mix for 8 minutes on low speed. While the motor is running, add the softened butter. Continue mixing for another 2–3 minutes or until all the butter is combined and the dough forms a smooth ball. Transfer to a lightly oiled bowl and set aside in a warm place for 1 hour, or until the dough has doubled in size.

On a lightly floured work surface, roll out the dough until it is 1 cm (½ inch) thick. Using a round cookie or donut cutter, cut 12–14 rounds. Use an apple corer to punch out a hole in the centre of each donut. Put the dough rings on a lightly floured sheet of baking paper. Cover loosely with plastic wrap and set aside for another 30–40 minutes, or until the dough rings are nice and puffed up and have doubled in size again.

In a heavy-based saucepan, heat the vegetable shortening to 170–180°C (340–350°F), or until a cube of bread dropped into the shortening turns golden brown in 15 seconds. Fry the donuts for about 50 seconds on each side. Remove and let cool on a wire rack, then glaze with one of the following recipes and eat with coffee!

1¼ tablespoons **dried yeast**

1 **egg**

600 g (1 lb 5 oz/4 cups) **plain (all-purpose) flour**

1 tablespoon **sugar**

125 ml (4 fl oz/½ cup) **milk,** at room temperature

½ teaspoon **salt**

2 teaspoons **natural vanilla extract**

40 g (1½ oz) softened **butter**

vegetable shortening or **Copha** for frying

RUBY GRAPEFRUIT DONUTS

Makes *12–14* donuts

Whisk together the grapefruit, grapefruit juice, icing sugar and 1 teaspoon of the milk in a bowl. If you would like the glaze to be a little thinner, add 1 more teaspoon of milk. Dip the donuts in the glaze and serve.

2 teaspoons chopped **ruby grapefruit**

2 tablespoons **ruby grapefruit juice**

125 g (4½ oz/1 cup) **icing (confectioners') sugar**

1–2 teaspoons **milk**

1 quantity **Donuts** (see above)

CHOC' MINT DONUTS

Makes *12–14* donuts

Whisk together the egg white and icing sugar until combined. Add the food dye and the peppermint essence and continue to whisk until you can drizzle lines of the mixture, using a spoon, which don't instantly disappear back into the mixture. If the mixture is too runny, add a touch more sugar.

Fill a piping bag with the mixture and use a size 1 mm (¹⁄₁₆ in) nozzle to pipe long lines onto baking paper. Let the lines dry overnight.

When the mixture has set, cut the lines into small peppermint sprinkles.

Melt the chocolate in a heat-proof bowl placed over a saucepan of simmering water.

Dunk the donuts in the melted chocolate then scatter over the peppermint sprinkles.

1 **egg white**

250 g (9 oz/2 cups) **icing (confectioners') sugar**

1 teaspoon **green food dye**

2 teaspoons **natural peppermint extract**

150 g (5¹⁄₂ oz) **dark cooking chocolate**

1 quantity **Donuts** (pages 206–7)

RASPBERRY CREAM DONUTS

Makes *12-14* donuts

Using an electric mixer, combine the butter, cream cheese, vanilla extract, 60 g (2 oz/½ cup) of the icing sugar and 60 ml (2 fl oz/¼ cup) water for about 1 minute, or until combined.

In a bowl, crush the raspberries with a whisk. Slowly incorporate the remaining icing sugar until smooth.

Spread the cream mixture onto the donuts with a rubber spatula.

Drizzle on the raspberry mixture.

Recipe note: Alternatively, the raspberry mixture could be used as a simple fruit glaze.

15 g (½ oz) **unsalted butter**

75 g (2¾ oz) **cream cheese**

¼ teaspoon **natural vanilla extract**

155 g (5½ oz/1¼ cups) **icing (confectioners') sugar**

30 g (1 oz/¼ cup) **raspberries**

1 quantity **Donuts** (pages 206–7)

LAMINGTON DONUTS

Makes *12-14* donuts

I like to use cheap cooking chocolate for this. I feel it gets the best result and doesn't overpower the airy yeast donut. Traditionally lamingtons don't have jam, but I think a little in the bullseye really pops it off. Be sure to get a low-quality chocolate but a high-quality raspberry jam.

Melt the chocolate in a heat-proof bowl placed over a saucepan of simmering water. Alternatively, put the chocolate in a bowl and microwave on high (100%) in three 10-second bursts, stirring after each burst, until the chocolate has just melted.

Dunk the donuts in the chocolate. I like to get good coverage all over – kinda like on a lamington. Place the covered donuts on a wire rack to cool slightly then sprinkle with the coconut and add a teaspoon of raspberry jam to the centre.

150 g (5½ oz) **dark cooking chocolate**, broken into small pieces

1 quantity **Donuts** (use round donuts instead of donut rings) (pages 206–7)

15 g (½ oz) **desiccated (shredded) coconut**

raspberry jam to serve

INDEX

ACKNOWLEDGEMENTS

I would like to thank everyone that has helped me along the way. Peace to all the people I have cooked with, rapped with, hustled clothes and mixed tapes with, took photos of, painted walls with, skateboarded and even hit a golf ball with. So many people ... My life has taken lots of turns so far and I really appreciate everyone that has been down. Even if our meetings were brief, you are all important to me.

To my wife Beci, you are the best. I know sometimes it just seems stupid, but if we don't try we will never know. Big love to my boys Ari and Tyke. Lots of love to Nanny, Mum, Rudin, Brooke, Zedrin, Johann, Andie and Chris.

Special thanks to Camilo and Karen from Cookie, Andrew and Meredith from Darkwave, Phil Ransom, Martin and Louise Mcintosh, Marg' and Erwin, Jeff Jank, Karla and Maurice, Elska Sandor, Jeff and Fawn, Annie and Norm, Damien at Village Bakery, Nino and Joes' butcher, Oranges and Lemons, Fireworks Foods, El Cielo Tortillas, City of Moreland, and the Wizards' Council.

Thanks to Paul McNally, Lucy Heaver and all the team at Hardie Grant; Tin and Ed for their amazing artwork throughout the book; Aileen Lord for all the great work on the layout; Sophie from Shiko for hand-making all the plates that Tin and Ed painted; Shane Beazley for helping me cook all the dishes in the book, thanks chef; Lauren Bamford for great photos and being down to work it out on the fly; Deb' Kaloper, cheers for taking my simple food so seriously and making it look awesome.

Thanks to those who helped out at the parties we threw for this book including: Ricky Do, Mark Campbell, Meelee Soorkia, Mia Mala, Tim Hillier, Aaron Woods, Dan Auselbrook, Laila Sakini, Kit Palaskas, Jo Miranda, Alice Oehr, Kirra Jamison, Guy Roseby, Max and Rosie, Conor and Amanda, Ed and Olivia, Baker D. Chirico, Rex for the music and Matt Skinner for all the great wine.

To all the staff who have jumped in the trucks over the years, I applaud all of you for giving it a try and stepping into the unknown with me.

To the guys who I text at all times of the day with recipe ideas: Jo Siahann, Attila Yilmaz, Pat Breen and Danny Garcia, cheers for the bounce.

Thanks also to Todd Wagstaff, for showing me the taco that changed my life; Van Do, for all your hard work and continued support, you are like the sister I never had; Mike Hoyle, for keeping me on track; James Fryman, not long 'til the philosophy truck; Brian Taranto, for the continued push and support and for the belief; Sebastian Hampson, for showing me to get fit you must exercise everyday.

Finally, thanks to all our customers; we wouldn't be here without you.

Published in 2014 by Hardie Grant Books

Hardie Grant Books (Australia)
Ground Floor, Building 1
658 Church Street
Richmond, Victoria 3121
www.hardiegrant.com.au

Hardie Grant Books (UK)
Dudley House, North Suite
34–35 Southampton Street
London WC2E 7HF
www.hardiegrant.co.uk

A Cataloguing-in-Publication entry is available from the catalogue of the National
Library of Australia at www.nla.gov.au

Hungry For That
ISBN: 978 1 74270 716 7

Publishing Director: Paul McNally
Managing Editor: Lucy Heaver
Editors: Meelee Soorkia and Ariana Klepac
Design Manager: Mark Campbell
Designer: Aileen Lord
Photographer: Lauren Bamford
Artwork supplied by Tin and Ed
Stylist: Deborah Kaloper
Production Manager: Todd Rechner
Production Assistant: Carly Milroy

Colour reproduction by Splitting Image Colour Studio

Printed in China by 1010 Printing International Limited

Find this book on **Cooked.**

cooked.com.au
cooked.co.uk